Income Inequality

Other Books of Related Interest:

Opposing Viewpoints Series

Bankruptcy

Global Sustainability

Impact of the Tech Giants

Working Women

At Issue Series

Corporate Corruption

How Valuable Is a College Degree?

Manufacturing Jobs in the US

Poverty in America

The Wealth Divide

Current Controversies Series

Poverty and Homelessness

Social Security

The Wage Gap

"Congress shall make
no law . . . abridging
the freedom of speech,
or of the press."

First Amendment to the US Constitution

The basic foundation of our democracy is the First Amendment guarantee of freedom of expression. The Opposing Viewpoints series is dedicated to the concept of this basic freedom and the idea that it is more important to practice it than to enshrine it.

Income Inequality

Noël Merino, Book Editor

GREENHAVEN PRESS
A part of Gale, Cengage Learning

GALE
CENGAGE Learning·

Farmington Hills, Mich • San Francisco • New York • Waterville, Maine
Meriden, Conn • Mason, Ohio • Chicago

GALE
CENGAGE Learning·

Judy Galens, *Manager, Frontlist Acquisitions*

For more information, contact:
Greenhaven Press
27500 Drake Rd.
Farmington Hills, MI 48331-3535
Or you can visit our Internet site at gale.cengage.com

For product information and technology assistance, contact us at

Gale Customer Support, 1-800-877-4253
For permission to use material from this text or product, submit all requests online at www.cengage.com/permissions

Further permissions questions can be emailed to permissionrequest@cengage.com

Articles in Greenhaven Press anthologies are often edited for length to meet page requirements. In addition, original titles of these works are changed to clearly present the main thesis and to explicitly indicate the author's opinion. Every effort is made to ensure that Greenhaven Press accurately reflects the original intent of the authors. Every effort has been made to trace the owners of copyrighted material.

Cover Image copyright © Mopic/Shutterstock.com.

LIBRARY OF CONGRESS CATALOGING-IN-PUBLICATION DATA

Income inequality / Noël Merino, Book Editor.
    pages cm. -- (Opposing viewpoints)
    Includes bibliographical references and index.
    ISBN 978-0-7377-7524-2 (hardcover) -- ISBN 978-0-7377-7525-9 (pbk.)
    1. Income distribution--United States. 2. Poverty--United States. 3. United States--Economic conditions. I. Merino, Noël, editor. II. Title.
    HC110.I5I477 2016
    339.2'2--dc23

                                                              2015024210

Printed in Mexico
1 2 3 4 5 6 7 19 18 17 16 15

Contents

Chapter 3: What Causes Income Inequality?

Why Consider
Opposing Viewpoints?

> "The only way in which a human being
> can make some approach to knowing the
> whole of a subject is by hearing what
> can be said about it by persons of every
> variety of opinion and studying all
> modes in which it can be looked at by
> every character of mind. No wise man
> ever acquired his wisdom in any mode
> but this."
>
> *John Stuart Mill*

In our media-intensive culture it is not difficult to find differing opinions. Thousands of newspapers and magazines and dozens of radio and television talk shows resound with differing points of view. The difficulty lies in deciding which opinion to agree with and which "experts" seem the most credible. The more inundated we become with differing opinions and claims, the more essential it is to hone critical reading and thinking skills to evaluate these ideas. Opposing Viewpoints books address this problem directly by presenting stimulating debates that can be used to enhance and teach these skills. The varied opinions contained in each book examine many different aspects of a single issue. While examining these conveniently edited opposing views, readers can develop critical thinking skills such as the ability to compare and contrast authors' credibility, facts, argumentation styles, use of persuasive techniques, and other stylistic tools. In short, the Opposing Viewpoints Series is an ideal way to attain the higher-level thinking and reading skills so essential in a culture of diverse and contradictory opinions.

In addition to providing a tool for critical thinking, Opposing Viewpoints books challenge readers to question their own strongly held opinions and assumptions. Most people form their opinions on the basis of upbringing, peer pressure, and personal, cultural, or professional bias. By reading carefully balanced opposing views, readers must directly confront new ideas as well as the opinions of those with whom they disagree. This is not to argue simplistically that everyone who reads opposing views will—or should—change his or her opinion. Instead, the series enhances readers' understanding of their own views by encouraging confrontation with opposing ideas. Careful examination of others' views can lead to the readers' understanding of the logical inconsistencies in their own opinions, perspective on why they hold an opinion, and the consideration of the possibility that their opinion requires further evaluation.

Evaluating Other Opinions

To ensure that this type of examination occurs, Opposing Viewpoints books present all types of opinions. Prominent spokespeople on different sides of each issue as well as well-known professionals from many disciplines challenge the reader. An additional goal of the series is to provide a forum for other, less known, or even unpopular viewpoints. The opinion of an ordinary person who has had to make the decision to cut off life support from a terminally ill relative, for example, may be just as valuable and provide just as much insight as a medical ethicist's professional opinion. The editors have two additional purposes in including these less known views. One, the editors encourage readers to respect others' opinions—even when not enhanced by professional credibility. It is only by reading or listening to and objectively evaluating others' ideas that one can determine whether they are worthy of consideration. Two, the inclusion of such viewpoints encourages the important critical thinking skill of objectively evaluating an author's credentials and bias. This evaluation will illuminate an author's reasons for taking a particular stance on an issue and will aid in readers' evaluation of the author's ideas.

It is our hope that these books will give readers a deeper understanding of the issues debated and an appreciation of the complexity of even seemingly simple issues when good and honest people disagree. This awareness is particularly important in a democratic society such as ours in which people enter into public debate to determine the common good. Those with whom one disagrees should not be regarded as enemies but rather as people whose views deserve careful examination and may shed light on one's own.

Thomas Jefferson once said that "difference of opinion leads to inquiry, and inquiry to truth." Jefferson, a broadly educated man, argued that "if a nation expects to be ignorant and free . . . it expects what never was and never will be." As individuals and as a nation, it is imperative that we consider the opinions of others and examine them with skill and discernment. The Opposing Viewpoints series is intended to help readers achieve this goal.

David L. Bender and Bruno Leone,
Founders

Introduction

"Economists disagree on just how much
inequality there is in America and how
best to measure it."

—Drew DeSilver,
Pew Research Center

The issue of income inequality is a controversial one. Debates abound as to whether income inequality is a problem, what exactly causes economic inequality, and what—if anything—should be done about it. Even the issue of how to measure income inequality is not without disagreement.

The most common way to measure inequality is to look at the Gini index, sometimes called the Gini coefficient. The Gini index varies from 0 to 1, where 0 indicates perfect income equality across all households. A 1, therefore, indicates perfect inequality, which would occur if one household had all the income and the rest of the households had no income. Of course, in the United States, the number is always somewhere between 0 and 1, with a higher number indicating greater inequality. The Gini index provides a snapshot of inequality, but looking at whether the Gini index is going up or down indicates whether income inequality is increasing or decreasing.

The US Census Bureau collects information about the income and wealth of US households. Household income includes all income of all people fifteen years and older in the household, regardless of whether they are related. Income can include wages or earnings; unemployment or worker's compensation; Social Security or other retirement income; survivor, disability, or veterans benefits; interest, dividends, and royalties; educational assistance or other assistance from outside the household; alimony and child support; and any other form of income. Household income does not include noncash benefits such as food stamps, health benefits, or subsidized housing.

Disparity in income has existed in the United States since its founding. Yet, the overall economic well-being of US households and the median income have changed over time, as has the level of inequality. In 2013 the median household income (with half of incomes above and half below) in the United States was $51,939, whereas in 1970 it was $46,759 (in 2013 dollars). However, the peak during those years was in 1998, when median income reached $56,895. In 2013, at the low end, 12.7 percent of households had incomes under $15,000, whereas at the high end, 10.1 percent of households had incomes of $150,000 or more.

The Gini index also has changed over time in the United States. In 1970 the Gini index of income inequality was 0.357. The Gini index has been on a fairly steady upward trajectory since then. In 1990 the Gini index was 0.406 and by 2013 had climbed to 0.459.

The Gini index, of course, does not tell the full story about a country's economic well-being. A poor country may have a low Gini index and a rich country may have a high Gini index. Yet, when looking at the Gini indexes of countries worldwide (as cited by the Central Intelligence Agency's *World Factbook*), patterns emerge: Most European countries have a Gini index below 0.35. Almost all the countries with a Gini index below 0.30 are in Europe. Most countries with a Gini index above 0.45 are in Africa or South America. Other countries with a Gini index similar to that of the United States include Jamaica, Bulgaria, Peru, Uruguay, the Philippines, Cameroon, Guyana, and Iran.

Using the Gini index to compute income inequality is not without detractors, and criticism about how income is measured often arises. Gary Burtless of the Brookings Institution notes,

The main problem with this income measure is that it only reflects households' before-tax cash incomes. It fails to account for changing tax burdens and the impact of income sources that do not take the form of cash. This means, for example, that tax cuts in 2001–2003 and 2008–2012 are missed in the census statistics. Even worse, the Census Bureau measure ignores income received as in-kind benefits and health insurance coverage from employers and the government.

Burtless contends that when such benefits and burdens are taken into account, middle-class incomes are higher and wealthy incomes are lower, thus decreasing the Gini index. Even if the number may vary according to how one computes income, what no one would deny is that income inequality *has* grown in the United States over the last several decades, even if the degree to which it exists is in question.

A lack of consensus pervades many of the issues surrounding income inequality in America. *Opposing Viewpoints: Income Inequality* explores many of these issues in chapters titled "Is Income Inequality in the United States a Problem?," "How Do Gender, Race, and Ethnicity Affect Income?," "What Causes Income Inequality?," and "What Should Be Done About Income Inequality?" This volume provides insight into the extent of income inequality in the United States, the causes, and the solutions.

CHAPTER 1

Is Income Inequality in the United States a Problem?

Chapter Preface

In the last few years in the United States, following the Great Recession, the topic of income inequality has been one of great debate. President Barack Obama discussed the issue in a speech on December 4, 2013, expressing his view that inequality has become a problem. He said,

> The combined trends of increased inequality and decreasing mobility pose a fundamental threat to the American Dream, our way of life, and what we stand for around the globe. And it is not simply a moral claim that I'm making here. There are practical consequences to rising inequality and reduced mobility.

President Obama claimed that rising inequality alongside decreased levels of upward mobility are harming the economy, decreasing social cohesion, and impeding democracy. Furthermore, he claimed that the recent changes in the economy harm everyone: "poor and middle class; inner city and rural folks; men and women; and Americans of all races."

Not all Americans agree with President Obama, and the response to the issue does tend to fall along party lines to a certain degree. Yet, there is a surprising amount of agreement about the existence of a problem (although certainly not about the solution). According to a Gallup poll conducted a month after the speech by President Obama, a majority of Americans of all political stripes expressed dissatisfaction with the way income and wealth are distributed in the United States. Among the adults polled, 39 percent were very dissatisfied with the way income and wealth are distributed in the United States, and 28 percent were somewhat dissatisfied. Only 7 percent of Americans were very satisfied with income and wealth distribution, and a quarter were somewhat satisfied.

Although 67 percent of all Americans expressed some degree of dissatisfaction with income and wealth distribution, differences existed based on political party. Democrats expressed the most dissatisfaction, with 75 percent saying they were either very dissatisfied or somewhat dissatisfied. Independents were just behind Democrats, with 70 percent expressing dissatisfaction. Although the number of Republicans expressing dissatisfaction was lower than both Democrats and Independents, a majority—54 percent—were dissatisfied with distribution of income and wealth.

Bringing in the issue of upward mobility, when Gallup asked people in the same poll about how satisfied they were with the opportunity for a person in the United States to get ahead by working hard, 61 percent of Republicans expressed some level of satisfaction, compared with 60 percent of Democrats and only 45 percent of Independents.

A strong majority of Americans do share the view that something is wrong with the current income and wealth distribution while also being largely satisfied with the opportunity to get ahead by working hard. Yet, there is no absolute agreement on whether the current levels of income inequality in the United States are acceptable, as authors of the viewpoints in this chapter illustrate.

*"Income inequality in the United States
has been rising for decades."*

Income Inequality Is
Higher in the United States
than Elsewhere

Steven J. Markovich

In the following viewpoint, Steven J. Markovich argues that income inequality in the United States has grown in recent decades and is now higher than in any other developed nation, with less class mobility than almost all other developed countries. He claims that the poverty rate has risen and the number of Americans needing social program support is high. Markovich contends that although there is no consensus about the causes of income inequality, globalization, de-unionization, technological change, and declining income tax rates have likely contributed. Markovich is a contributing editor at the Council on Foreign Relations.

As you read, consider the following questions:

1. According to Markovich, the average real after-tax household income of the top 1 percent of American earners grew by what percentage from 1979 to 2007?

2. According to the author, 80 percent of economic experts agree that the leading reason for rising US income inequality is what?

3. Markovich claims that what percentage of those born into the lowest income quintile will stay there?

Income inequality in the United States, measured by the standard Gini coefficient, is substantially higher than that of almost any other developed nation, and even some developing countries such as Russia and India. Popular anger over inequality peaked in the autumn 2011 Occupy Wall Street protests [against social and economic inequality], which catalyzed similar movements internationally. President [Barack] Obama followed a December 2013 speech on economic mobility with further discussion of policy ideas in his 2014 State of the Union speech, titled "Opportunity for All."

There are many complex causes of income inequality. Certainly, globalization and technological change have led to greater competition for lower-skilled workers—many of whom have also lost union membership—while giving well-educated, higher-skilled workers increased leverage. Changes to tax rates, including favorable treatment for capital gains, may also play a role.

Rising U.S. Income Inequality

According to the Congressional Budget Office, income inequality in the United States has been rising for decades, with the top echelon of earners rapidly outpacing the rest of the population. The average real after-tax household income of the top 1 percent rose 275 percent from 1979 to 2007. Meanwhile, income for the remainder of the top quintile (81st to 99th percentile) grew 65 percent. Income for the majority of the population in the middle of the scale (21st through 80th percentiles) grew just 37 percent for the same period. And the bottom quintile experienced the least growth income at just 18 percent.

Furthermore, in 1965, a typical corporate CEO [chief executive officer] earned more than twenty times a typical worker; by 2011, the ratio was 383:1, according to the Economic Policy Institute.

Still, this view is not universal among experts. An August 2012 paper by the Hoover Institution of Stanford argued that income inequality is not rising when noncash benefit programs are taken into account.

While many of the suspected drivers of rising income inequality—globalization, technological change and the rising value of education—affect other nations as well, few have seen as stark a rise in inequality as the United States. From 1968 to 2010, the share of national income earned by the top 20 percent rose from 42.6 to 50.2 percent, with gains concentrated at the very top. Meanwhile, the "middle class," the middle 60 percent, saw its share decline from 53.2 to 46.5 percent. This increasing income inequality is captured by the steady rise in the U.S. Gini coefficient, from 0.316 in the mid-1970s to 0.378 in the late 2000s. Today, the U.S. income distribution is one of the most uneven among major developed nations.

Globalization and De-Unionization

Economic forces underlie the growth of income inequality. Highly skilled workers have greatly benefited from worldwide opportunities, from the star actor whose movies reach a global audience to the entrepreneur who can quickly and cheaply bring a new product to market through Chinese contract manufacturing.

Meanwhile, globalization has brought tough competition to other American workers who have seen jobs move overseas, wages stagnate, and unions decline. The median union member earns roughly a quarter more than a nonunion counterpart. Forty years ago, a quarter of private sector workers were represented by unions, but today it is only 6.9 percent. Despite a workforce one-fifth of the size, the public sector has more union members.

Immigration likely plays a role in stagnant wages, especially among workers without a high school degree, of which immigrants make up about half. One study found that a 10 percent increase in the local immigrant population correlated with a 1.3 percent decline in the price of labor-intensive services, but it is difficult to disentangle this competitive effect from others on the labor market.

Free-trade advocate Alan Blinder says that while beneficial for the United States as a whole, the increased labor competition from globalization will be painful for many Americans. He advocated for helping displaced workers through a stronger safety net, reforming education, and encouraging innovation and entrepreneurship. Fellow Princeton economist Paul Krugman believes that "we need to restore the bargaining power that labor has lost over the last thirty years, so that ordinary workers as well as superstars have the power to bargain for good wages."

Education and Technological Change

Most high wages come from high-skill jobs that require a commensurate level of education. After decades of gradually narrowing, the college wage premium has grown dramatically since 1980, as the annual growth in the college-educated workforce (2 percent) failed to keep pace with rising demand (3.27 to 3.66 percent) driven by technological change. In 2011, the median earnings of a worker with a bachelor's degree were 65 percent higher than a high school graduate's; holders of professional degrees (MD, JD, MBA) enjoyed a 161 percent premium. Higher educational attainment correlates both with higher earnings and lower unemployment.

However, college degrees do not guarantee good jobs. Falling costs in communications and computers are leading to the offshoring and automation of some jobs that were once the purview of well-paid professionals, from scientists in pharmaceutical labs to finance and accounting jobs. There is a widening wage premium between those with advanced degrees and those with a bachelor's degree only. Since the 2000s, the wage premium for those with only a four-year degree has remained flat, while it has continued to grow for those with advanced degrees.

Gary S. Becker and Kevin M. Murphy of the University of Chicago see education as the major driver of rising income inequality: "In the United States, the rise in inequality accompanied a rise in the payoff to education and other skills. We believe that the rise in returns on investments in human capital is beneficial and desirable, and policies designed to deal with inequality must take account of its cause." To address income inequality, they argue for policies that would increase the percentages of American youth who complete high school and college and against making the tax code more progressive.

In a 2012 survey, 80 percent of economic experts agreed that a leading reason for rising U.S. income inequality was that technological change has affected workers with some skill sets differently than others, but not all prominent economists agree. James K. Galbraith believes that "the skills bias argument—the notion that inequality is being driven by technological change and education and the supply of skills—is comprehensively rebutted by the evidence." He argues instead that the credit cycle has concentrated income in specific sectors, such as finance, tech, and real estate.

Income Tax Rates

One tool for addressing income inequality is a more progressive tax code. While some argue that shifting some money from the rich to the poor means that money can be used to create more social utility—the economic concept of declining marginal utility—others see this shift as unfair and unwise because it reduces the ability of more productive citizens to reinvest in the skills and businesses responsible for their higher relative income, thus retarding overall growth. While economic models and theories can attempt to quantify the relationship between inequality and growth, the optimum balance cannot be empirically determined.

The United States has generally cut top income tax rates over the past half century. When John F. Kennedy entered the White House in 1961, the top ordinary income tax bracket, applied to wages and savings interest, was more than 90 percent. Ronald Reagan slashed the top rate from 70 percent in 1981 to 28 percent after 1986. Tax increases under the first President [George H.W.] Bush and President [Bill] Clinton brought the top rate to 39.6 percent, but tax cuts signed by President George W. Bush and reauthorized by President Obama set it to 35 percent.

Tax rates on investment income in the form of capital gains taxes and dividends have also declined, with the current rate of 15 percent the lowest since 1933. Investment income ultimately is derived from the after-tax profits of corporations, whose tax rate has also declined since the [President Dwight D.] Eisenhower era from more than 50 percent to today's marginal rate of 35 percent. Corporate income tax has declined steadily as a share both of corporate profits and as a percentage of GDP [gross domestic product] over the past half century.

The Social Security payroll tax, which funds both old-age pensions and Medicare, is regressive because it is a flat rate

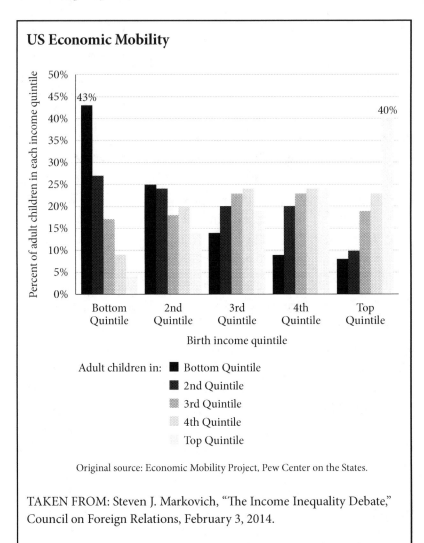

US Economic Mobility

Percent of adult children in each income quintile

50%
45% 43%
40%
35%
30%
25%
20%
15%
10%
5%
0%

40%

Bottom Quintile   2nd Quintile   3rd Quintile   4th Quintile   Top Quintile

Birth income quintile

Adult children in: ■ Bottom Quintile
■ 2nd Quintile
▨ 3rd Quintile
▨ 4th Quintile
□ Top Quintile

Original source: Economic Mobility Project, Pew Center on the States.

TAKEN FROM: Steven J. Markovich, "The Income Inequality Debate," Council on Foreign Relations, February 3, 2014.

that only applies to the first $110,100 of wages (as of 2012). On the other hand, roughly half of U.S. taxpayers pay no additional federal income tax.

A Tax Policy Center analysis of all federal taxes found overall progressive taxation, with each quartile paying a successively higher rate and the top 0.1 percent paying an effective rate of 30.4 percent. While higher than the 14.1 percent borne by the middle quartile, 30.4 percent is lower than the historical rates paid by this small group, which is earning its largest share of national income since the Great Depression.

Social Program Support

The poverty rate tends to generally follow the economic cycle. As the economy reached new heights in 2000, the poverty rate fell to 11.1 percent—a rate not seen since 1973—but in 2010 the poverty rate had risen to 15.1 percent.

Under President Lyndon Johnson's Great Society, most assistance was in the form of cash benefits to needy families. Through the 1970s and 1980s, noncash benefit programs were created or accelerated, including college grants, food stamps, and housing assistance. The 1990s ushered in welfare reform, replacing federal cash assistance with TANF [Temporary Assistance for Needy Families] block grant to states, with work requirements and time limits. The refundable earned income tax credit (created in 1975) was greatly expanded at this time, providing extra cash to workers in an effort to "make work pay."

Today, record numbers receive food stamps, and one in five Americans struggle to afford food. The five-year farm bill passed in late January 2014 by the House—with Senate approval expected—contains a 1 percent cut to the food stamp program ($8 billion over 10 years), through tighter restrictions on heating assistance. The number of Social Security Disability Insurance recipients has surged by more than 22 percent since the recession began in 2007; that program effectively acts as a long-term unemployment benefit for some.

From Medicaid to unemployment benefits, many social support programs are driven by decisions at the state level. States have less flexibility to run deficits, and many have cut programs to needy citizens. Pennsylvania recently joined other states in eliminating its general assistance program.

U.S. Economic Mobility

Many Americans take pride in the belief that everyone has a chance to "make it big," and rags-to-riches stories are almost legends. But today, more than 40 percent of those born into the lowest income quintile will stay there, and less than 30 percent will make an above-average income.

Harvard's Equality of Opportunity Project issued a paper based on tax record data for taxpayers born between 1971 and 1993, and determined that there has not been a significant change in intergenerational mobility. The researchers found that while stable, the level of upward mobility in the United States is not uniform; some regions consistently offer less economic mobility. Common factors that correlated with regions with more mobility were: less segregation, less income inequality, better schools, greater social capital, and more stable families. Still, while income mobility may be stable in a relative sense, inequality is growing in an absolute sense. The gaps between the median incomes in each quintile have grown as higher incomes grew at a faster rate.

Among developed countries, only the United Kingdom has less class mobility than the United States; in 2006, the Brookings Institution found that 47 percent of U.S. parents' income advantages are passed to their children, greater than in France (41 percent), Germany (32 percent) or Sweden (27 percent). The countries with the highest mobility were Canada, Norway, Finland and Denmark, where less than 20 percent of economic advantages are passed to children.

President Obama's 2014 State of the Union address did not use the term "income inequality," and his proposals focused on broadly expanding economic opportunity. His plan to raise the federal minimum wage to $10.10 an hour for all workers would require congressional action; economists still debate whether minimum wage increases do more harm than good by lowering employment as wages rise. Many of the president's ideas concerned accelerating economic growth as a way to increase opportunity. For instance, he stressed the importance of access to a quality education by highlighting programs such as universal pre-K and universal broadband access and proposed efforts to get universities to improve access for low-income students.

The Pew Research Center found the percentage of adults self-identifying as middle class has declined from 53 percent in 2008 to 44 percent in 2014. While large majorities of both major political parties say the gap between rich and poor has increased in the last ten years, there is sharp disagreement over whether the government should act to reduce the gap. International investors and economists see income inequality as a drag on economic growth.

| "America's inequality distorts our soci-
| ety in every conceivable way."

Growing Inequality Is a Serious Social Problem

Joseph E. Stiglitz

In the following viewpoint, Joseph E. Stiglitz argues that wealth in America has become too concentrated in the top 1 percent. He contends that the growth in wealth of the rich, along with a decrease in wealth of the middle class, has caused severe inequality that has several negative effects. Stiglitz claims that the rich have influenced policy in such a way that the inequality is now self-perpetuating and threatens to result in social unrest. Stiglitz is an economist, a professor at Columbia University, and the author of The Price of Inequality: How Today's Divided Society Endangers Our Future.

As you read, consider the following questions:

1. Stiglitz claims that the top 1 percent have seen their incomes rise by what percentage over the past decade?

2. What does the author say is the most obvious example of a policy created by the top 1 percent for the top 1 percent?

3. What fraction of Americans are on food stamps, according to the author?

It's no use pretending that what has obviously happened has not in fact happened. The upper 1 percent of Americans are now taking in nearly a quarter of the nation's income every year. In terms of wealth rather than income, the top 1 percent control 40 percent. Their lot in life has improved considerably. Twenty-five years ago, the corresponding figures were 12 percent and 33 percent. One response might be to celebrate the ingenuity and drive that brought good fortune to these people and to contend that a rising tide lifts all boats. That response would be misguided. While the top 1 percent have seen their incomes rise 18 percent over the past decade, those in the middle have actually seen their incomes fall. For men with only high school degrees, the decline has been precipitous—12 percent in the last quarter-century alone. All the growth in recent decades—and more—has gone to those at the top. In terms of income equality, America lags behind any country in the old, ossified Europe that President George W. Bush used to deride. Among our closest counterparts are Russia with its oligarchs and Iran. While many of the old centers of inequality in Latin America, such as Brazil, have been striving in recent years, rather successfully, to improve the plight of the poor and reduce gaps in income, America has allowed inequality to grow.

Economists long ago tried to justify the vast inequalities that seemed so troubling in the mid-19th century—inequalities that are but a pale shadow of what we are seeing in America today. The justification they came up with was called "marginal-productivity theory." In a nutshell, this theory associated higher incomes with higher productivity and a greater contribution to society. It is a theory that has always been cherished by the rich. Evidence for its validity, however, remains thin. The corporate executives who helped bring on the recession of the past three years—whose contribution to our society, and to their own companies, has been massively negative—went on to receive large bonuses. In some cases, companies were so embarrassed about calling such rewards "performance bonuses" that they felt compelled to change the name to "retention bonuses" (even if the only thing being retained was bad performance). Those who have contributed great positive innovations to our society, from the pioneers of genetic understanding to the pioneers of the information age, have received a pittance compared with those responsible for the financial innovations that brought our global economy to the brink of ruin.

The Problems with Inequality

Some people look at income inequality and shrug their shoulders. So what if this person gains and that person loses? What matters, they argue, is not how the pie is divided but the size of the pie. That argument is fundamentally wrong. An economy in which *most* citizens are doing worse year after year—an economy like America's—is not likely to do well over the long haul. There are several reasons for this.

First, growing inequality is the flip side of something else: shrinking opportunity. Whenever we diminish equality of opportunity, it means that we are not using some of our most valuable assets—our people—in the most productive way possible. Second, many of the distortions that lead to inequality—such as those associated with monopoly power and preferential tax treatment for special interests—undermine the efficiency of the economy. This new inequality goes on to create new distortions, undermining efficiency even further. To give just one example, far too many of our most talented young people, seeing the astronomical rewards, have gone into finance rather than into fields that would lead to a more productive and healthy economy.

Third, and perhaps most important, a modern economy requires "collective action"—it needs government to invest in infrastructure, education, and technology. The United States and the world have benefited greatly from government-sponsored research that led to the Internet, to advances in public health, and so on. But America has long suffered from an underinvestment in infrastructure (look at the condition of our highways and bridges, our railroads and airports), in basic research, and in education at all levels. Further cutbacks in these areas lie ahead.

None of this should come as a surprise—it is simply what happens when a society's wealth distribution becomes lop-sided. The more divided a society becomes in terms of wealth, the more reluctant the wealthy become to spend money on common needs. The rich don't need to rely on government for parks or education or medical care or personal security—they can buy all these things for themselves. In the process, they become more distant from ordinary people, losing whatever empathy they may once have had. They also worry about strong government—one that could use its powers to adjust the balance, take some of their wealth, and invest it for the common good. The top 1 percent may complain about the kind of government we have in America, but in truth they like it just fine: too gridlocked to redistribute, too divided to do anything but lower taxes.

The Power of the Top 1 Percent

Economists are not sure how to fully explain the growing inequality in America. The ordinary dynamics of supply and demand have certainly played a role: laborsaving technologies have reduced the demand for many "good" middle-class, blue-collar jobs. Globalization has created a worldwide marketplace, pitting expensive unskilled workers in America against cheap unskilled workers overseas. Social changes have also played a role—for instance, the decline of unions, which once represented a third of American workers and now represent about 12 percent.

But one big part of the reason we have so much inequality is that the top 1 percent want it that way. The most obvious example involves tax policy. Lowering tax rates on capital gains, which is how the rich receive a large portion of their income, has given the wealthiest Americans close to a free ride. Monopolies and near monopolies have always been a source of economic power—from John D. Rockefeller at the beginning of the last century to Bill Gates at the end. Lax enforcement of antitrust laws, especially during Republican administrations, has been a godsend to the top 1 percent. Much of today's inequality is due to manipulation of the financial system, enabled by changes in the rules that have been bought and paid for by the financial industry itself—one of its best investments ever. The government lent money to financial institutions at close to 0 percent interest and provided generous bailouts on favorable terms when all else failed. Regulators turned a blind eye to a lack of transparency and to conflicts of interest.

When you look at the sheer volume of wealth controlled by the top 1 percent in this country, it's tempting to see our growing inequality as a quintessentially American achievement—we started way behind the pack, but now we're doing inequality on a world-class level. And it looks as if we'll be building on this achievement for years to come, because what made it possible is self-reinforcing. Wealth begets power, which begets more wealth. During the savings-and-loan scandal of the 1980s—a scandal whose dimensions, by today's standards, seem almost quaint—the banker Charles Keating was asked by a congressional committee whether the $1.5 million he had spread among a few key elected officials could actually buy influence. "I certainly hope so," he replied. The Supreme Court, in its recent *Citizens United [v. Federal Election Commission]* case, has enshrined the right of corporations to buy government, by removing limitations on campaign spending. The personal and the political are today in perfect alignment. Virtually all U.S. senators, and most of the representatives in the House, are members of the top 1 percent when they arrive, are kept in office by money from the top 1 percent, and know that if they serve the top 1 percent well they will be rewarded by the top 1 percent when they leave office. By and large, the key executive-branch policy makers on trade and economic policy also come from the top 1 percent. When pharmaceutical companies receive a trillion-dollar gift—through legislation prohibiting the government, the largest buyer of drugs, from bargaining over price—it should not come as cause for wonder. It should not make jaws drop that a tax bill cannot emerge from Congress unless big tax cuts are put in place for the wealthy. Given the power of the top 1 percent, this is the way you would *expect* the system to work.

The Costs Imposed on Society

America's inequality distorts our society in every conceivable way. There is, for one thing, a well-documented lifestyle effect—people outside the top 1 percent increasingly live beyond their means. Trickle-down economics may be a chimera, but trickle-down behaviorism is very real. Inequality massively distorts our foreign policy. The top 1 percent rarely serve in the military—the reality is that the "all-volunteer" army does not pay enough to attract their sons and daughters, and patriotism goes only so far. Plus, the wealthiest class feels no pinch from higher taxes when the nation goes to war: borrowed money will pay for all that. Foreign policy, by definition, is about the balancing of national interests and national resources. With the top 1 percent in charge, and paying no price, the notion of balance and restraint goes out the window. There is no limit to the adventures we can undertake;

corporations and contractors stand only to gain. The rules of economic globalization are likewise designed to benefit the rich: They encourage competition among countries for *business*, which drives down taxes on corporations, weakens health and environmental protections, and undermines what used to be viewed as the "core" labor rights, which include the right to collective bargaining. Imagine what the world might look like if the rules were designed instead to encourage competition among countries for *workers*. Governments would compete in providing economic security, low taxes on ordinary wage earners, good education, and a clean environment—things workers care about. But the top 1 percent don't need to care.

Or, more accurately, they think they don't. Of all the costs imposed on our society by the top 1 percent, perhaps the greatest is this: the erosion of our sense of identity, in which fair play, equality of opportunity, and a sense of community are so important. America has long prided itself on being a fair society, where everyone has an equal chance of getting ahead, but the statistics suggest otherwise: The chances of a poor citizen, or even a middle-class citizen, making it to the top in America are smaller than in many countries of Europe. The cards are stacked against them. It is this sense of an unjust system without opportunity that has given rise to the conflagrations in the Middle East: rising food prices and growing and persistent youth unemployment simply served as kindling. With youth unemployment in America at around 20 percent (and in some locations, and among some sociodemographic groups, at twice that); with one out of six Americans desiring a full-time job not able to get one; with one out of seven Americans on food stamps (and about the same number suffering from "food insecurity")—given all this, there is ample evidence that something has blocked the vaunted "trickling down" from the top 1 percent to everyone else. All of this is having the predictable effect of creating alienation—voter turnout among those in their 20s in the last election stood at 21 percent, comparable to the unemployment rate.

In recent weeks we have watched people taking to the streets by the millions to protest political, economic, and social conditions in the oppressive societies they inhabit. Governments have been toppled in Egypt and Tunisia. Protests have erupted in Libya, Yemen, and Bahrain. The ruling families elsewhere in the region look on nervously from their air-conditioned penthouses—will they be next? They are right to worry. These are societies where a minuscule fraction of the population—less than 1 percent—controls the lion's share of the wealth; where wealth is a main determinant of power; where entrenched corruption of one sort or another is a way of life; and where the wealthiest often stand actively in the way of policies that would improve life for people in general.

The Future of America

As we gaze out at the popular fervor in the streets, one question to ask ourselves is this: When will it come to America? In important ways, our own country has become like one of these distant, troubled places.

Alexis de Tocqueville [a French political thinker] once described what he saw as a chief part of the peculiar genius of American society—something he called "self-interest properly understood." The last two words were the key. Everyone possesses self-interest in a narrow sense: I want what's good for me right now! Self-interest "properly understood" is different. It means appreciating that paying attention to everyone else's self-interest—in other words, the common welfare—is in fact a precondition for one's own ultimate well-being. Tocqueville was not suggesting that there was anything noble or idealistic about this outlook—in fact, he was suggesting the opposite. It was a mark of American pragmatism. Those canny Americans understood a basic fact: Looking out for the other guy isn't just good for the soul—it's good for business.

The top 1 percent have the best houses, the best educations, the best doctors, and the best lifestyles, but there is one thing that money doesn't seem to have bought: an understanding that their fate is bound up with how the other 99 percent live. Throughout history, this is something that the top 1 percent eventually do learn. Too late.

> *"We should collectively be pleased by increases in income at the top, so long as they were not caused by taking . . . from individuals at the bottom."*

Income Inequality Is Not a Problem

Richard A. Epstein

In the following viewpoint, Richard A. Epstein argues that there is no reason to be opposed to income inequality or wealth inequality unless gains by the rich are harming the poor. Epstein claims that overall economic growth benefits everyone, even if it does produce greater inequality. He argues against tax increases and an increased minimum wage as policies aimed at decreasing inequality, claiming that such policies will harm everyone. Epstein is the Laurence A. Tisch Professor of Law at the New York University School of Law.

As you read, consider the following questions:

1. According to Epstein, what is a Pareto improvement?

2. Epstein contends that marginal tax rates at the federal level reached what percentage under President Herbert Hoover's Revenue Act of 1932?

3. The author claims that in a weak economy, a minimum wage increase is likely to cause the greatest job losses among what group of workers?

One month into the second term [February 2013] of the [President Barack] Obama administration, the economic prognosis looks mixed at best. On growth, the U.S. Department of Commerce reports the last quarter of 2012 produced a small decline in gross domestic product, without any prospects for a quick reversal. On income inequality, the most recent statistics (which only go through 2011) focus on the top 1 percent.

"Incomes Flat in Recovery, but Not for the 1%" reports Annie Lowrey of the *New York Times*. Relying on a recent report prepared by the well-known economist Professor Emmanuel Saez, who is the director for the Center for Equitable Growth at [the University of California,] Berkeley, Lowrey reports that the income of the top 1 percent has increased by 11.2 percent, while the overall income of the rest of the population has decreased slightly by 0.4 percent.

A Pareto Improvement

What should we make of these numbers? One approach is to stress the increase in wealth inequality, deploring the gains of the top 1 percent while lamenting the decline in the income of the remainder of the population. But this approach is only half right. We should be uneasy about any and all income declines, period. But, by the same token, we should collectively be pleased by increases in income at the top, so long as they were not caused by taking, whether through taxation or regulation, from individuals at the bottom.

This conclusion rests on the notion of a Pareto improvement, which favors any changes in overall utility or wealth that make at least one person better off without making anyone else worse off. By that measure, there would be an unambiguous social improvement if the income of the wealthy went up by 100 percent so long as the income of those at the bottom end did not, as a consequence, go down. That same measure would, of course, applaud gains in the income of the 99 percent so long as the income of the top 1 percent did not fall either.

This line of thought is quite alien to thinkers like Saez, who view the excessive concentration of income as a harm even if it results from a Pareto improvement. Any center for "equitable growth" has to pay as much attention to the first constraint as it does to the second. Under Saez's view of equity, it is better to narrow the gap between the top and the bottom than to increase the overall wealth.

To see the limits of this reasoning, consider two hypothetical scenarios. In the first, 99 percent of the population has an average income of $10 and the top 1 percent has an income of $100. In the second, we increase the income gap. Now, the 99 percent earn $12 and the top 1 percent earns $130. Which scenario is better?

This hypothetical comparison captures several key points. First, *everyone* is better off with the second distribution of wealth than with the first—a clear Pareto improvement. Second, the gap between the rich and the poor in the second distribution is greater in both absolute and relative terms.

The Problem with Equality

The stark challenge to ardent egalitarians is explaining why anyone should prefer the first distribution to the second. Many will argue for some intermediate solution. But how much wealth are they prepared to sacrifice for the sake of equality? Beyond that, they will have a hard time finding a political mechanism that could achieve a greater measure of equality and a program of equitable growth. The public choice problems, which arise from self-interested intrigue in the political arena, are hard to crack.

These unresolved tensions are revealed by looking at a passage from Saez's report "Striking It Richer." Saez is largely indifferent to these problems of implementation when he observes ominously that

> "falls in income concentration due to economic downturns are temporary unless drastic regulation and tax policy changes are implemented and prevent income concentration from bouncing back. Such policy changes took place after the Great Depression during the New Deal and permanently reduced income concentration until the 1970s. In contrast, recent downturns, such as the 2001 recession, led to only very temporary drops in income concentration.
>
> The policy changes that are taking place coming out of the Great Recession (financial regulation and top tax rate increase in 2013) are not negligible but they are modest relative to the policy changes that took place coming out of the Great Depression. Therefore, it seems unlikely that US income concentration will fall much in the coming years."

Let's unpack this. It is surely true that the top 1 percent (or at least the top 1 percent of that 1 percent) is heavily invested in financial instruments, and thus will suffer a decline in income with the regulation of the financial markets. But by the same token, it would be absurd to praise any declines in overall capital wealth because of its supposed contribution to greater equality for all individuals. Nor would it make any sense to describe, as Saez does, the current situation as one of "booming stock-prices" when the Dow Jones Industrial Average still teeters below its 2007 high. Take into account inflation and one finds that the real capital stock of the United States has actually declined over the last six years, which reduces the wealth available to create private sector jobs.

The Benefits of Inequality

Yes, the top 1 percent make a lot of money. They also pay a lot in taxes and make up a vastly disproportional share of charitable giving. They work long hours and are entrepreneurial risk-takers.

It has been claimed by the Left for some time now that inequality is bad in and of itself. The real question remains unanswered, however: Is inequality permissible if all people's lives are improving? If all people are making economic gains, would liberals destroy that progress in the name of equality?

Dustin Siggins,
"Wealth and Inequality on YouTube,"
National Review, *March 27, 2013.*

Nor, moreover, is there anything permanent about the 2012 gain in income at the top. As Saez himself notes, some portion of the recent income surge has resulted from a "retiming of income," by which high-income taxpayers accelerate income to 2012 to avoid the higher 2013 tax rates. Accordingly, we can expect that real incomes at the top will be lower in 2013 than otherwise would have been the case. Indeed, it is possible that these "modestly" higher taxes could produce the worst of both worlds, by depressing government revenues *and* reducing the income of the rich.

Saez's own qualification is best read as a backhanded recognition of the perverse incentives that rapid changes in the tax structure create. It is a pity that he does not go one step further to accept the sound position that low, flat, and steady tax rates offer the only way—the only equitable way—to sustainable overall growth.

A Leveling Down

Unfortunately, Saez would rather move our system precisely in the opposite direction. He praises the dramatic shifts that took place during the Great Depression, when marginal tax rates at the federal level reached 62 percent under [President Herbert] Hoover's Revenue Act of 1932, and stayed high during [President Franklin D.] Roosevelt's New Deal period. The anemic economic performance of the Roosevelt New Deal arose in large part from a combination of high taxation and destructive national policies that strangled free trade, increased union power, and reduced overall agricultural production. Today, Saez concentrates on the income growth of the top 1 percent. He does not address the feeble levels of economic growth over the last five years.

Saez may think that the latest round of tax increases and financial regulations are "modest" in the grand scheme of things. But their effects have been predictable. The declines in productivity have translated into lower levels of income and well-being for all affected groups.

The blunt truth remains that any government-mandated leveling in society will be a leveling *down*. There is no sustainable way to make the poor richer by making the rich poorer. But increased regulation and taxation will make both groups poorer. Negative growth hardly becomes equitable if a larger fraction of the decline is concentrated at the top earners.

The Middle Class and the Minimum Wage

The effort to promote equitable growth at the expense of the top 1 percent has serious consequences for current policy. It is no accident that in his recent State of the Union address, President Obama once again called for increases in taxes on "the wealthiest and the most powerful." If adopted, these changes would make the tax system more progressive and the economy more sluggish.

Indeed the president goes further. He pushes for the adoption of other wrongheaded policies that would also hurt the very people whom they are intended to help. Consider that the Lowrey story featured a picture of President Obama appearing before a crowd at the Linamar Corporation in Arden, N.C., seeking to make good on his promise to raise the minimum wage to $9.00—to advance, of course, the interests of the middle class to whom the president pays undying allegiance.

The president thinks he can redistribute income without stifling economic growth. The simple rules of supply and demand dictate that any increase in the minimum wage that expands the gap between the market wage and the statutory wage will increase the level of unemployment. The jobs that potential employees desperately need will disappear from the marketplace. In a weak economy, a jump in the minimum wage is likely, as the *Wall Street Journal* has noted, to reduce total jobs, with unskilled minority workers bearing the brunt of the losses.

Unfortunately, the president displays his resolute economic ignorance by proclaiming, "Employers may get a more stable workforce due to reduced turnover and increased productivity." But they can get that stability benefit unilaterally, without new legislation that throttles other employers for whom the proposition is false. Only higher productivity secures long-term higher wages.

Indeed, the best thing the president could do is to just get out of the way. After over four years of his failed policies, Mortimer Zuckerman reports that unemployment rates still hover at 8 percent, and 6.4 million fewer people have jobs today than in 2007. That's an overall jobs decline of 4.9 percent in the face of a population growth of 12.5 million people from July 2007 to July of 2012. The same period has registered sharp increases in the number of people on disability insurance (to 11 million people) and food stamps (to some 48 million).

45

There is a deep irony in all of these dismal consequences. The president's State of the Union address targeted the plight of the middle class. That appeal always makes political sense—but it also makes for horrific economic policy. All too often, the calls for equitable growth yield anything but the desired outcome.

Rather than focus on "equitable growth," the president should focus on flattening the income tax and deregulating labor markets. Today's constant emphasis on progressive taxation and government intervention in labor markets will continue to lead the country, especially the middle class, on a downward path.

> *"The rise of income inequality and
> wealth inequality are intimately con-
> nected, and cause all sorts of problems
> over the long term."*

Inequality Is a Problem for Middle-Class and Low-Income Workers

Sean McElwee

*In the following viewpoint, Sean McElwee argues that rising in-
come inequality has led to a problematic growth in wealth inequality. McElwee claims that this rising income and wealth inequality is caused by an unfair tax system and could be partially
corrected by higher tax rates on the rich. McElwee contends that
the growing inequality in wealth has had a negative effect on democracy, concentrating political power in the hands of the rich.
McElwee is a research associate at Demos, a public policy organization.*

As you read, consider the following questions:

1. According to McElwee, the richest 0.1 percent of Americans controlled what percentage of the nation's wealth in 2012?

2. McElwee claims that despite what some Republicans claim, high levels of inequality have what effect on economic growth?

3. The author claims that one solution to reduce the influence the wealthy are having on the political system is to reduce what?

Bold prediction: Rising inequality of income and wealth will be the most important political battleground over the next few decades.

Inequality of Income and Wealth

Just take a look at the figures. The share of income accruing to the top 1 percent increased from 9 percent in 1976 to 20 percent in 2011. The richest 0.1 percent controlled 7 percent of the wealth in 1979 and 22 percent of the wealth in 2012. Meanwhile, there are a number of studies out there showing that the most effective way to reduce this inequality would be higher taxes on income and wealth, but the rich won't let it happen.

Consider also this: The rise of income inequality and wealth inequality are intimately connected, and cause all sorts of problems over the long term. As Emmanuel Saez and Gabriel Zucman write,

> Income inequality has a snowballing effect on the wealth distribution: Top incomes are being saved at high rates, pushing wealth concentration up; in turn, rising wealth inequality leads to rising capital income concentration, which contributes to further increasing top income and wealth shares.

That is, income is a flow, which quickly becomes a stock. The rich make enough money to save; in contrast middle-class and low-income workers don't have enough money to live, so they are increasingly burdened by debt. They can't build up wealth, which means they are deprived of opportunity. This creates a self-perpetuating cycle of wealth on the top and debt on the bottom.

In a comedy bit on wealth, Chris Rock claims, "You can't get rid of wealth." The empirical research on the question largely supports his assertion. In *The Son Also Rises*, Gregory Clark finds that wealth remains in a family for 10 to 15 generations and notes,

> Groups that seem to persist in low or high status, such as the black and the Jewish populations in the United States, are not exceptions to a general rule of higher intergenerational mobility. They are experiencing the same universal rates of slow intergenerational mobility as the rest of the population.

An Unfair Tax System

But, of course wealth and income inequality weren't always as bad as they are today. What happened? In a word: cheating. Although many people try to explain rising inequality away by arguing we live in a winner-take-all economy or that inequality is the result of skill-biased technological change, these arguments are bunk. Inequality has been driven by public policy choices that favored the rich, the decline of unions and the rise of finance. . . . Tax rates on both income and inheritance were high during the relatively equal '60s, '70s and '80s and then fell dramatically paving the way for the inequality we see today.

The best way to reduce inequality would be to tax income and wealth. While conservatives often claim that this would reduce economic growth, such claims have very little economic support. For instance, Thomas Piketty, Emmanuel Saez

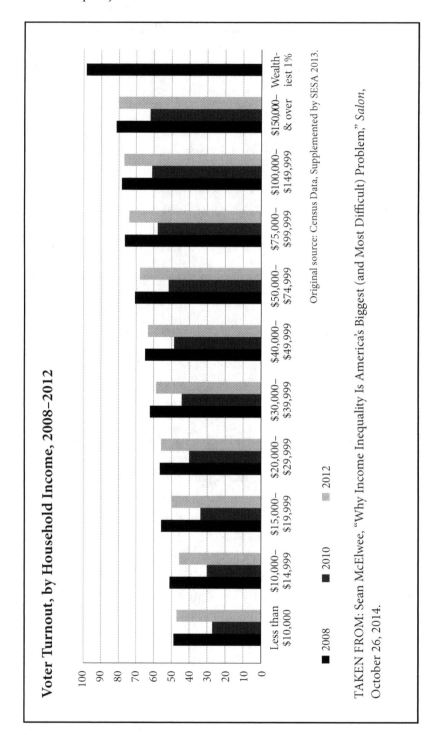

Voter Turnout, by Household Income, 2008–2012

■ 2008   ■ 2010   ▒ 2012

Less than $10,000 | $10,000–$14,999 | $15,000–$19,999 | $20,000–$29,999 | $30,000–$39,999 | $40,000–$49,999 | $50,000–$74,999 | $75,000–$99,999 | $100,000–$149,999 | $150,000 & over | Wealthiest 1%

Original source: Census Data. Supplemented by SESA 2013.

TAKEN FROM: Sean McElwee, "Why Income Inequality Is America's Biggest (and Most Difficult) Problem," *Salon*, October 26, 2014.

and Stefanie Stantcheva find no correlation between economic growth and tax cuts. Because of this, they find, "the top tax rate could potentially be set as high as 83%."

Nobel Prize winner Peter Diamond argues that the top marginal tax rate could safely breach 73 percent, and indeed, such a rate might even be "optimal." Another recent study finds the top marginal tax rate could be as high as 90 percent. Republicans sometimes claim that inequality is necessary for economic growth; in fact, the evidence suggests rather the opposite is true: High levels of inequality imperil growth.

But, here's the problem: The same political forces that allowed the 1 percent to take our political system hostage have only worsened in the past decade. As Nick Hanauer notes in a recent Intelligence Squared debate,

> At the same time, the percent of—of labor—the percent of GDP [gross domestic product] devoted to labor has gone from 52 to 42. So that difference is about a trillion dollars annually. So that—here's the thing you have to understand. That trillion dollars isn't profit because it needs to be or should be or has to be. It's profit because powerful people like me and [Edward Conrad] prefer it to be. That trillion dollars could very easily be spent on wages. Or—or on discounts for consumers. This isn't a consequence of some magical law of economics. This is a consequence of differentials in power.

The Concentration of Political Power

Nick hits on a very important point: The rising concentration of economic power has coincided with a concentration of political power. A recent paper by Adam Bonica and others illustrates that as inequality has increased, the rich have spent more money on the political system.

As Benjamin Page, Larry Bartels and Jason Seawright recently found, the wealthy tend to be more economically conservative than the population at large. But a particularly startling finding is that "on economic issues wealthy Democratic respondents tended to be more conservative than Democrats in the general population." The wealthy are using the political system to turn their income into wealth and then that wealth into more wealth. They're going to keep doing it, unless we stop them. One solution is to reduce the massive turnout gap between the rich and poor.

Studies show that states with more low-income turnout have higher minimum wages, more generous child health insurance programs and stricter anti-predatory lending policies. They also have more generous welfare benefits. The fight against inequality will be a long one, but the first step is turning out to vote—the most radical step one can take in our country is actually believing democracy is more than just an idea.

> "Over the past one-, two-, and three-
> decade periods, both middle-class and
> poor households have experienced no-
> ticeable gains in living standards."

Income Inequality Is Not
a Problem for the Poor and
Middle Class

Gary Burtless

*In the following viewpoint, Gary Burtless argues that despite all
the talk of income inequality, the data show that middle-class
and poor households have fared well in recent decades. Burtless
contends that although it is true that the wealthiest Americans
had the largest income increases in recent years, they also have
suffered the largest losses. Burtless claims that the tax system and
government programs protect low- and moderate-income families from such large losses. Burtless is a senior fellow in economic
studies and the John C. and Nancy D. Whitehead Chair at the
Brookings Institution.*

As you read, consider the following questions:

1. According to Burtless, what has happened to pretax and after-tax incomes since 2000 for Americans in the bottom 90 percent of income distribution?

2. The author claims that from 1979 to 2010, the middle three-fifths of households in the income distribution experienced what percentage of growth in after-tax incomes?

3. Burtless contends that from 1980 to 2010 in-kind and health insurance benefits increased by what percentage of middle-class after-tax income?

Last month [December 2013] the Congressional Budget Office [CBO] published new estimates of the distribution of federal tax burdens. CBO analysts assembled updated information on Americans' incomes to calculate household tax burdens between 1979 and 2010. They also predicted 2013 tax burdens based on projections of income combined with a careful reading of current tax law.

Income Losses During the Great Recession

Some crucial findings of the new study may come as a surprise, especially to people who believe incomes of the poor and middle class have stagnated since the turn of the century as incomes at the top have soared. The CBO's latest numbers show the opposite is true. Since 2000 pretax and after-tax incomes have improved among Americans in the bottom 90% of the income distribution. Among Americans in the top 1% of the distribution, real incomes sank.

To be sure, the pre- and posttax incomes of the top 1% improved in 2010 compared with 2009 while incomes in the bottom 90% of households remained essentially flat. Thus, almost all the net income gains in 2010 went to people at the very top. 2010 was the first year of the current recovery, and a disproportionate share of income gains in the early recovery was concentrated on the well-to-do. Income reports published by the IRS [Internal Revenue Service] suggest this trend continued in 2011 and 2012, when the most affluent taxpayers continued to enjoy big income gains. The flip side is that Americans at the top of the distribution also saw the biggest percentage losses in their incomes during the Great Recession [referring to the U.S. recession that lasted from December 2007 to June 2009, and the ensuing global recession]. CBO's new numbers show that households in the top income percentile saw their before- and after-tax incomes shrink more than one-third between 2007 and 2009. Middle-income Americans experienced pretax income losses of 4.5% and after-tax income losses of just 1.4%. In the bottom one-fifth of U.S. households, after-tax incomes actually edged up during the recession.

The market incomes of Americans up and down the income distribution were badly hurt by the Great Recession. (Market income consists of wages and other labor compensation, business income of the self-employed, interest, dividends, capital gains, rent payments to individuals, and private pension payments.) Many households are a long way from recovering the market income losses they suffered in the recession. As it happens, households at the top of the income distribution are among families in this situation. Even accounting for the robust pretax gains they enjoyed in 2010–2012, IRS data suggest the top 1% of households had lower pretax incomes in 2012 than they did in 2007 . . . or in 2000.

The tax system and government transfers shelter American households from part of the market income losses they suffer in a recession. Unemployment benefits replace some of the wages lost as a result of a layoff. Social Security, Medicaid, and Medicare replace part of the compensation lost by older and disabled workers when they are forced to leave the workforce in a weak job market. The progressive income tax reduces households' tax liabilities more than proportionately when Americans experience a drop in their wages or business income. The stimulus measures adopted in the Great Recession boosted the income protection provided by the government. In percentage terms, government protection against recession-fueled income losses was much more effective in 2008–2010 for low- and moderate-income families than it was for those in the top 1%.

Income Gains in Recent Decades

Over longer time horizons and measured over full business cycles the latest CBO numbers confirm that the income gains of the top 1% have been considerably faster than those enjoyed by middle-income Americans. For example, between 1979 and 2010 the after-tax real incomes of the top 1% tripled. Households in the middle three-fifths of the income distribution saw their after-tax incomes grow only about 40%. What the CBO statistics do not show, however, is that middle- and low-income families have failed to share in the nation's long-term prosperity. Over the past one-, two-, and three-decade periods, both middle-class and poor households have experienced noticeable gains in living standards. Their gains are slower than those experienced by middle-income families in the earlier postwar era, but the gains are well above zero.

One reason that many observers miss these income gains is that the nation's most widely cited income statistics do not show them. A commonly used indicator of middle-class income is the Census Bureau's estimate of median household money income. Measured in constant dollars, median household income reached a peak in 1999 and fell 9% in the years thereafter. The main problem with this income measure is that it only reflects households' before-tax cash incomes. It fails to account for changing tax burdens and the impact of income sources that do not take the form of cash. This means, for example, that tax cuts in 2001–2003 and 2008–2012 are missed in the Census statistics. Even worse, the Census Bureau's measure ignores income received as in-kind benefits and health insurance coverage from employers and the government.

The new CBO income statistics show the growing importance of these items. In 1980, in-kind benefits and employer and government spending on health insurance accounted for just 6% of the after-tax incomes of households in the middle one-fifth of the distribution. By 2010 these in-kind income sources represented 17% of middle-class households' after-tax income. The income items missed by the Census Bureau are increasing faster than the income items included in its money income measure.

The broadest and most accurate measures of household income are published by the CBO. CBO's newest estimates confirm the long-term trend toward greater inequality, driven mainly by turbocharged gains in market income at the very top of the distribution. The market incomes of the top 1% are extraordinarily cyclical, however. They soar in economic expansions and plunge in recessions. Income changes since 2007 fit this pattern. What many observers miss, however, is the success of the nation's tax and transfer systems in protecting low- and middle-income Americans against the full effects of a depressed economy. As a result of these programs, the spendable incomes of poor and middle-class families have been better insulated against recession-driven losses than the incomes of Americans in the top 1%. As the CBO statistics demonstrate, incomes in the middle and at the bottom of the distribution have fared better since 2000 than incomes at the very top.

> "Though the politically correct on both
> sides are loath to admit it, income in-
> equality is beautiful."

The Life Enhancing, Unrelenting Brilliance of Income Inequality

John Tamny

In the following viewpoint, John Tamny argues that an increase in the wealth gap is a positive sign that the lifestyle gap between rich and poor is quickly shrinking. Tamny claims that promise of vastly unequal income and wealth is what drives great inventions and pushes forward advancements for all members of society. Tamny claims that politicians should stop lamenting economic inequality and avoid intervening with the markets. Tamny is political economy editor at Forbes *and editor of RealClear Markets.com.*

As you read, consider the following questions:

1. Tamny claims that income inequality would only matter to a small degree if what were true?

2. Tamny claims that the billions in wealth of Apple Inc. cofounder Steve Jobs reduced the lifestyle gap in what two ways?

3. For what reason does the author claim the lifestyle gap failed to shrink in terms of homeownership?

If there's one thing that's certain about media coverage of periods when a Republican is in the White House, it's that copious amounts of ink will be spilled decrying "rising levels of income inequality" that allegedly threaten our economic health. The assertions are economically bankrupt, but what's interesting now is that some on the right are now using the same illogic to bash the [President Barack] Obama economy.

That there's much to criticize Obama for is to state the obvious, but income inequality should not enter the discussion.

The Benefits of Income Inequality

Lost on the economic illiterates that populate both sides of the commentariat is the simple, life-enhancing truth that when the wealth gap is increasing, that's a certain signal that the *lifestyle gap* is shrinking—*rapidly*. Though the politically correct on both sides are loath to admit it, income inequality is beautiful.

Most readers are at this point familiar with the arguments in favor of wealth differentials, but for those new to the discussion, here are some of them:

- Income inequality would only matter to a small degree if the proverbial team picture of America's rich were a static one. That it's not is a happy reality that both sides dare not mention, but if the fluid nature of rich is doubted, readers need only visit a library in order to peruse various copies of the Forbes 400 over the decades to see that the 400 is a club that constantly adds and subtracts members.

- Importantly, if we didn't have income inequality we'd have to invent it. As McGill University economist Reuven Brenner pointed out so brilliantly in his essential book *History: The Human Gamble*, it is gaps in wealth that drive creativity among the citizenry. Seeing the immense wealth possessed by the most successful, those not in the rich club strive mightily to join the wealthy; their innovations redounding to individuals of all income classes.

- Luxury is a historical phenomenon. The baubles of the rich merely predict what we'll all have if politicians do not erect barriers to production. The best example of this is the cell phone. Back in the early '90s individuals walking while talking on wireless phones were a source of awe, and to some degree ridicule about the plastic nature of Beverly Hills. The great Christopher Buckley had a running joke about cell phone use (for it being so rare) in his classic novel *Thank You for Smoking*. Fast-forward twenty years, and to walk the streets of any city in the U.S. is to see Americans of all income classes listening to music, texting, searching Internet sites, and watching television on small rectangular objects that also serve as the once much-coveted wireless phone.

The Social Value of Wealth

Thinking about wealth creation in the U.S. and the ever-growing wealth gap, Apple Inc. cofounder Steve Jobs died worth billions; his staggering wealth a signal that he'd greatly reduced the lifestyle gap. Music that used to be expensive, and that required the buyer to purchase much that was unwanted, now costs .99 cents. Wireless phones that were once the obscure property of the superrich are now positively pedestrian.

Patrick Soon-Shiong made his billions for inching us ever closer to the still distant cure for cancer. Soon-Shiong's com-

The Economic Pie

Greater inequality might actually increase the size of the economic pie rather than shrink it. . . . If economic growth is strong enough—enlarging the pie by a sufficient amount—then even though the slices going to the poor and the middle class are comparatively skinnier, they still end up with more pie.

Scott Winship,
"Income Inequality Is Good for the Poor,"
Federalist, *November 5, 2014.*

pany developed a drug that invades cancerous cells only to kill those cells once the invasion is complete. Figure John D. Rockefeller in the early part of the 20th century spent $500,000 to unsuccessfully find a cure for a grandson who ultimately died of scarlet fever. Today, Americans of all income classes don't even consider the once fatal disease; Rockefeller's ability to at least fund the initial fight against it having resulted from his unrelenting and successful efforts to democratize access to reading light (kerosene), and then eventually the petroleum that made Americans already relentless amid abundance even more mobile.

Naysayers will point to billionaire John Paulson and argue that his billions are the result of his having profited from the inability of financially strapped Americans to stay current on their mortgages. The latter is a very simplistic argument. In truth, Paulson's billions provided to the marketplace precious signals telling investors that further commitment of capital to the housing space would prove destructive. In short, Paulson's financial success was a big positive for an economy always limited by access to growth capital.

The Meddling of Politicians

If the above is not enough, it must be remembered about Paulson that, if the markets had been allowed to work their magic, that his successful bet against housing would have very much reduced the lifestyle gap that is always the certain result of economic achievement. Indeed, Paulson's successful investments foretold what could have been a severe correction in the housing market that would have enabled prudent Americans to achieve the dream of homeownership on the cheap; that is, assuming politicians had gotten out of the way and allowed overextended sellers to put their homes up for sale.

Instead, the very politicians who express fear about income inequality expropriated the funds of the careful in our midst in order to paper over the mistakes of lenders and borrowers alike. The imprudent were bailed out on the backs of the prudent, and a lifestyle gap in terms of house that was set to shrink didn't reveal itself thanks to allegedly compassionate politicians. Not asked enough then or now is, what's compassionate about taking from the careful (I'm neither rich, nor do I own a home) in order to cushion the egregious errors of the prodigals in our midst?

So while expansions in the wealth gap have become sport for the partisan and economically illiterate on both sides of the political divide, the real truth is that the sentient among us should cheer every time they read of rising inequality. The sentient should cheer because it signals enterprise being rewarded, freedom to keep the fruits of one's labor, and then for all of us not rich it signals that our lives are getting better and better; the lifestyle disparity between us and them (the rich) shrinking precisely because economic achievement is taking place.

"Greater income inequality seems to amplify and intensify the effects of social status differentiation—bigger material differences creating bigger social distances."

Why Inequality Is Bad for You—and Everyone Else

Richard Wilkinson

In the following viewpoint, Richard Wilkinson argues that research supports the view that income inequality creates a wide range of social problems, including illness, violence, poor school performance, lower levels of social trust, more drug abuse, and high rates of imprisonment. Wilkinson claims that the negative effects harm not only the poor but also the vast majority of society. Wilkinson is cofounder of the Equality Trust, an organization in the United Kingdom that works to reduce economic inequality.

As you read, consider the following questions:

1. By what factor is the homicide rate of the United States greater than that of Japan, according to the author?

2. According to Wilkinson, approximately what percentage of the population would benefit from greater equality?

3. What is the social reason for eating together, according to the author?

People have always known that inequality is divisive and socially corrosive. What is surprising, now that we have the data to compare societies, is how clear the effects of inequality are.

The Negative Effects of Inequality

A wide range of social problems are worse in societies with bigger income differences between rich and poor. These include physical and mental illness, violence, low math and literacy scores among young people, lower levels of trust and weaker community life, poorer child well-being, more drug abuse, lower social mobility and higher rates of imprisonment and teenage births.

The differences in performance of more and less equal societies are often enormous: Most of these problems are between twice and ten times as common in countries like the United States, Britain and Portugal, which have large income differences compared to countries with smaller income differences like the Nordic countries or Japan. For example, taking high, medium and low inequality countries, the homicide rate in the United States in 2009 was 50 per million population compared with 18 in Canada and 5 in Japan.

The police, prisons and public services needed to defend ourselves against these problems are expensive and often not very effective. But the underlying causal processes are fairly clear. The problems that get worse when there is more inequality are all problems that become more common lower down the social ladder within each society.

Greater income inequality seems to amplify and intensify the effects of social status differentiation—bigger material differences creating bigger social distances. So the most common trigger to violence seems to be people feeling disrespected and looked down on. Although social class imprints its effects on us from earliest childhood onward, greater inequality makes these effects more marked.

The Benefits of Greater Equality

But inequality does not harm the poor alone. The effects are so large because almost everyone is affected. The benefits of greater equality are biggest at the bottom of society, but a number of studies suggest that a large majority—perhaps 90% or 95%—of the population benefits from greater equality.

We cannot say what happens to the superrich because they are a fraction of 1% of the population, and we do not have separate data on their health, violence or drug use. Because position in the hierarchy has always been important to well-being, we have an inherited sensitivity to social status that works rather like ranking systems among some monkeys. However, human beings have lived in every kind of society from the most egalitarian (such as the hunting and gathering societies of human prehistory) to the most tyrannical dictatorships.

Where there is more equality, we use more cooperative social strategies, but where there is more inequality, people feel they have to fend for themselves and competition for status becomes more important.

The Quality of Social Relationships

Crucially important is the quality of social relationships. Because members of the same species have the same needs, they can, all too easily, be each other's worst rivals—fighting for food, nesting sites, territories, sexual partners and so on. But human beings, as well as having the potential to be each other's most feared rivals and competitors, also have the opposite potential: We can be each other's best sources of cooperation, assistance, help, learning and love. Depending on our social relationships, other people can be the best—or the worst.

Of paramount importance in our social development was to avoid conflict and competition for basic necessities. That is why we eat together. It is also what the religious symbolism of communion is about. Whether society has great inequality and a strong status hierarchy, whether there is a strong sense of superiority and inferiority, tells us whether we are in the same boat together and depend on cooperation and reciprocity or whether we have to fend for ourselves in a dog-eat-dog society.

What matters is not simply adults' recognition of inequality and social status; it is also a matter of how the parental experience of adversity is passed on to children to affect their early development.

The sensitive period in early childhood that shapes development exists in many different species. Its function is to enable the young to adapt to the kind of environment they will have to deal with. Among human beings, that is primarily a matter of adapting to the social environment.

Are you growing up in a world where you will have to fight for what you can get, watch your back and learn not to trust others because we are all rivals, or are you growing up in a world where you will depend on cooperation, reciprocity and mutuality?

Periodical and Internet Sources Bibliography

The following articles have been selected to supplement the diverse views presented in this chapter.

Jared Bernstein	"The Impact of Inequality on Growth," Center for American Progress, December 2013.
Donald J. Boudreaux and Mark J. Perry	"Donald Boudreaux and Mark Perry: The Myth of a Stagnant Middle Class," *Wall Street Journal*, January 23, 2013.
Thomas L. Hungerford	"In Defense of the 99 Percent: Rising US Income Inequality—Causes, Consequences, and Solutions," *Dialogue*, Autumn 2013.
Stewart Lansley	"The Hourglass Society," *Los Angeles Review of Books*, May 28, 2013.
Aparna Mathur	"A Cell Phone in Every Pot," *National Review*, October 9, 2013.
Elizabeth McNichol, Douglas Hall, David Cooper, and Vincent Palacios	"Pulling Apart: A State-by-State Analysis of Income Trends," Center on Budget and Policy Priorities and Economic Policy Institute, November 15, 2012.
Ryan Messmore	"Justice, Inequality, and the Poor," *National Affairs*, no. 10, Winter 2012.
Pew Research Center	"The Lost Decade of the Middle Class: Fewer, Poorer, Gloomier," August 22, 2012.
Jonathan Rauch	"Inequality and Its Perils," *National Journal*, September 27, 2012.
Michael Tanner	"The Income-Inequality Myth," *National Review*, January 10, 2012.
Jordan Weissmann	"US Income Inequality: It's Worse Today than It Was in 1774," *Atlantic*, September 19, 2012.

CHAPTER 2

How Do Gender, Race, and Ethnicity Affect Income?

Chapter Preface

In the early 1960s, legislation was passed to enshrine in law the prohibition of wage disparity based on gender, race, and ethnicity. Yet, debate continues today about whether wage disparity based on gender, race, and ethnicity is a problem and whether further legislation is needed.

The Equal Pay Act of 1963 amended the Fair Labor Standards Act of 1938 with a new subsection:

> No employer . . . shall discriminate . . . between employees on the basis of sex by paying wages to employees . . . at a rate less than the rate at which he pays wages to employees of the opposite sex . . . for equal work on jobs the performance of which requires equal skill, effort, and responsibility, and which are performed under similar working conditions, except where such payment is made pursuant to (i) a seniority system; (ii) a merit system; (iii) a system which measures earnings by quantity or quality of production; or (iv) a differential based on any other factor other than sex.

An employee can bring a lawsuit against her employer if she is receiving different wages than male employees for equal work under equal conditions, requiring equal skill, effort, and responsibility. Title VII of the Civil Rights Act of 1964, passed a year later, codified the federal prohibition of discrimination on the basis of race, color, religion, sex, or national origin.

A recent lawsuit further expanded the rights of employees to bring lawsuits based on discrimination. Lilly Ledbetter worked for Goodyear Tire & Rubber Company from 1979 to 1998. Late in her career, she became aware that she had been paid less than her male counterparts for years. Ledbetter filed formal charges with the Equal Employment Opportunity Commission (EEOC) and filed a lawsuit charging pay discrimination under the Equal Pay Act and the Civil Rights Act. Her case culminated in a Supreme Court decision finding back pay and damages beyond those going back 180 days prior to her filing were not covered due to a statute of limitations on discrimination claims. This decision prompted the passage of the Lilly Ledbetter Fair Pay Act, which allows the 180-day statute of limitations to reset with each paycheck that is affected by past discrimination.

Despite these legal protections against discrimination in pay, some groups continue to push for further legislation. The National Women's Law Center (NWLC) supports the Paycheck Fairness Act, which would require stronger proof from employers to show differences in pay are not discriminatory and would strengthen penalties for equal pay violations. According to NWLC, the Paycheck Fairness Act would strengthen the Equal Pay Act:

> The change would put gender-based wage discrimination on an equal footing with discrimination based on race or ethnicity, for which full compensatory and punitive damages are already available.

However, critics of this proposed legislation, such as James Sherk and Rachel Greszler of the Heritage Foundation, argue that the new law

> would do little to combat discrimination. It would heavily burden both employers and employees with frivolous litigation. Employers would defend themselves by using uniform pay systems and uniform work schedules that ignore individual performance and individual preference. This uniformity would cut the pay and limit the flexibility of both men and women.

As this issue illustrates, the debate about income inequality is rife with disagreement about how much discrimination is a problem and how much existing legislation is addressing the issue.

> *"It is not necessary for progress in closing the wage gap to come at men's expense; it is only necessary that women's real earnings grow faster than men's."*

Gender, Race, and Ethnicity Negatively Affect Earnings

Ariane Hegewisch, Claudia Williams, Heidi Hartmann, and Stephanie Keller Hudiburg

In the following viewpoint, Ariane Hegewisch, Claudia Williams, Heidi Hartmann, and Stephanie Keller Hudiburg argue that there is a persistent earnings gap between men and women that, with slow progress, remains substantial. The authors contend that in addition to gender, race and ethnicity also play a role in creating income gaps. Hegewisch is a study director, Williams is a research analyst, Hartmann is president, and Keller Hudiburg is a research intern, all at the Institute for Women's Policy Research.

As you read, consider the following questions:

1. The authors contend that if the pace of change in the annual earnings ratio continues as it has since 1960, men and women will reach parity by what year?

2. What racial or ethnic group has the highest median weekly earnings, according to the authors, and what explanation is given for this?

3. According to the authors, women's real wages in 2012 are almost identical to their earnings in which previous year?

The gender wage gap in the United States has not seen significant improvement in recent years and remains a reality for women across racial and ethnic groups. In 2013, the ratio of women's to men's median weekly full-time earnings was 82.1 percent, an increase of more than one percentage point since 2012, when the ratio was 80.9 percent (but still slightly lower than the 2011 ratio of 82.2 percent). This corresponds to a weekly gender wage gap of 17.9 percent. Real earnings have remained largely unchanged since 2012; women's median weekly earnings increased by $5 to $706 in 2013; men's median weekly earnings increased to $860, a marginal increase of $7 compared with 2012.

The Gender Earnings Gap

Another measure of the earnings gap, the ratio of women's and men's median annual earnings for full-time year-round workers, was 76.5 in 2012 (data for 2013 are not yet available), the same ratio as in 2004. An earnings ratio of 76.5 means the annual gender wage gap for full-time year-round workers is 23.5 percent.

The annual gender earnings ratio for full-time year-round workers, which includes self-employed workers, tends to be slightly lower than the ratio for weekly earnings (which excludes the self-employed and includes full-time workers who work only part of the year). The two series exhibit the same general trend over the long term (even though they often move in different directions in the short term). Both earnings ratios are for full-time workers only; if part-time and part-year workers were included, the ratios of women's to men's earnings would be even lower, as women are more likely than men to work reduced schedules, often in order to manage child-rearing and other caregiving work.

Progress in closing the gender earnings gap, based on both weekly and annual earnings, has slowed considerably since the 1980s and early 1990s. Based on median weekly earnings, the gender earnings gap narrowed by only 1.7 percentage points during the last ten years (2004 to 2013); in the previous ten-year period (1994 to 2003), it narrowed by 3.1 percentage points, and during the ten years prior to that (1984 to 1993), by 9.7 percentage points. Based on median annual earnings, progress in closing the gender earnings gap has also slowed considerably. If the pace of change in the annual earnings ratio were to continue at the same rate as it has since 1960, it would take until 2058 for men and women to reach parity. . . .

The Impact of Race and Ethnicity

Women of all major racial and ethnic groups earn less than men of the same group and also earn less than white men. Hispanic workers have lower median weekly earnings than white, black and Asian workers, the lowest of any race/ethnic group shown. Hispanic women's median earnings were $541 per week of full-time work, only 61.2 percent of white men's median weekly earnings but 91.1 percent of the median weekly earnings of Hispanic men (because Hispanic men also have low earnings). The median weekly earnings of black women were $606, only 68.6 percent of white men's earnings but 91.3 percent of black men's median weekly earnings, which are also fairly low. Earnings for a full-time week of work leave His-

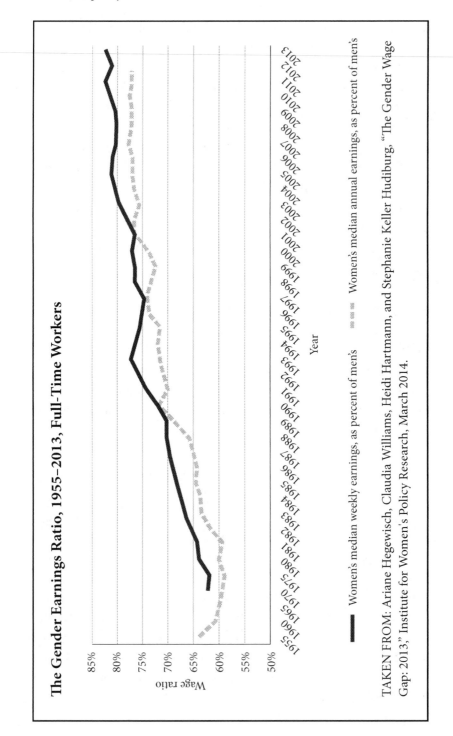

The Gender Earnings Ratio, 1955–2013, Full-Time Workers

Wage ratio

85%
80%
75%
70%
65%
60%
55%
50%

1955 1960 1965 1970 1975 1980 1981 1982 1983 1984 1985 1986 1987 1988 1989 1990 1991 1992 1993 1994 1995 1996 1997 1998 1999 2000 2001 2002 2003 2004 2005 2006 2007 2008 2009 2010 2011 2012 2013

Year

—— Women's median weekly earnings, as percent of men's ▪ ▪ ▪ Women's median annual earnings, as percent of men's

TAKEN FROM: Ariane Hegewisch, Claudia Williams, Heidi Hartmann, and Stephanie Keller Hudiburg, "The Gender Wage Gap: 2013," Institute for Women's Policy Research, March 2014.

panic women well below, and Hispanic men and black women not much above, the qualifying income threshold for receipt of food stamps of $588.75 for a family of four.

Primarily because of higher rates of educational attainment for both genders, Asian workers have higher median weekly earnings than white, black or Hispanic workers. Asian women's earnings are 92.6 percent of white men's earnings but only 73.3 percent of Asian men's earnings. White women earn 81.7 percent of what white men earn, very close to the ratio for all women to all men, because whites remain the largest group in the labor force.

Asian and Hispanic women were the only groups of women . . . who experienced significant gains in real earnings in 2013, of $38 (4.9 percent) for Asian women and $12 (1.9 percent) for Hispanic women. Black and white women saw no significant real earnings increase. All groups of men saw small increases (ranging from $7 to $11 per week). . . .

Closing the Wage Gap

The wage ratio increased in both the annual and weekly earnings series until the early 2000s. The real earnings columns (earnings adjusted to constant 2013 dollars so that the effect of inflation has been eliminated) show very different stories for women and men. Women's real earnings grew considerably from 1980, the first year shown for which we have data for both series, to 2000, from $30,136 to $37,146 in the annual series and from $559 to $685 in the weekly series (ending with 2002). During those same years, men's earnings fell, rose, fell, and rose again, ending in 2000 at $50,388 about the same place they were in 1980 in the annual series, and in 2002 at $879 in the weekly series, slightly below their value in 1980 at $885. The wage gap narrowed when women's real earnings were growing and men's were not.

It is not necessary for progress in closing the wage gap to come at men's expense; it is only necessary that women's real earnings grow faster than men's. After the early 2000s, women's real wages have also stagnated: in the annual series, earnings of $38,345 in 2012 are almost identical to 2001 earnings of $38,438; in the weekly series, women's earnings are $699 in 2003 compared with $706 in 2013. For men the stagnation continues: since these 2000 dates men's real earnings have stagnated at about $50,000 annually and about $870 weekly. The failure of women's real earnings to continue to grow in the 2000s while men's continued to stagnate is, of course, associated with almost no closing of the wage gap in this time period.

Ideally the wage gap would close when both women and men are making real wage gains, with women making greater gains. With the economy slowly recovering from the Great Recession [referring to the U.S. recession that lasted from December 2007 to June 2009, and the ensuing global recession], real wage gains should reappear. Yet, economists and other commentators have identified institutional and other changes in the U.S. economy that seem to make it less likely that the productivity gains the economy enjoys will be passed on to most workers in the form of higher real wages (recently only those at the very top have gained substantially). Women's earnings have become increasingly important to family incomes with the decline in marriage and the growth in single-mother and dual-earner families. The persistent gender earnings gap and the failure of real earnings to grow for the majority of working women and men expose many families to economic stress.

"Today's young women are the first in modern history to start their work lives at near parity with men."

The Gender Wage Gap Is Not as Extreme for Young Women

Pew Research Center

In the following viewpoint, the Pew Research Center contends that millennial women (those reaching adulthood around 2000) are experiencing greater income and workplace equality than women of prior generations. However, the author notes that there are still concerns about gender discrimination in the workplace, and time will tell whether choices about family and career will impact the future wage parity of these women. The Pew Research Center is a nonpartisan fact tank that informs the public about the issues, attitudes, and trends shaping America and the world.

As you read, consider the following questions:

1. What percentage of millennial young women say that they have been discriminated against at work because of their gender, according to the author?

2. According to the author, what percentage of employed workers with at least a bachelor's degree were women in 2012?

3. The author claims that according to federal statistics, the percentage of women in managerial and administrative positions increased by how many points from 1980 to 2012?

A new cohort of young women—members of the so-called millennial generation—has been entering the workforce for the past decade. At the starting line of their careers, they are better educated than their mothers and grandmothers had been—or than their young male counterparts are now. But when they look ahead, they see roadblocks to their success. They believe that women are paid less than men for doing the same job. They think it's easier for men to get top executive jobs than it is for women. And they assume that if and when they have children, it will be harder for them to advance in their careers.

While the public sees greater workplace equality between men and women now than it did 20 to 30 years ago, most believe more change is needed. Among millennial women, 75% say this country needs to continue making changes to achieve gender equality in the workplace, compared with 57% of millennial men. Even so, relatively few young women (15%) say they have been discriminated against at work because of their gender.

As millennial women come of age in the "lean in" era, they share many of the same views and values about work as their male counterparts. They want a job they enjoy that provides security and flexibility, and they place relatively little importance on high pay. At the same time, however, young working women are less likely than men to aspire to top management jobs: 34% say they are not interested in becoming a boss or top manager; only 24% of young men say the same. The gender gap on this question is even wider among working adults in their 30s and 40s, the age at which many women face the trade-offs that go with work and motherhood.

These findings are based on a new Pew Research Center survey of 2,002 adults, including 810 millennials (adults ages 18 to 32), conducted Oct. 7–27, 2013. The survey finds that, in spite of the dramatic gains women have made in educational attainment and labor force participation in recent decades, young women view this as a man's world—just as middle-aged and older women do. Roughly half of millennial women (51%) and their older counterparts (55%) say society favors men over women; just 6% of both groups say it favors women over men.

The survey findings are paired with a Pew Research analysis of census data that shows that today's young women are the first in modern history to start their work lives at near parity with men. In 2012, among workers ages 25 to 34, women's hourly earnings were 93% those of men. By comparison, among all working men and women ages 16 and older, women's hourly wages were 84% those of men. And women in the younger age cohort were significantly more likely than their male counterparts to have completed a bachelor's degree—38% versus 31% in 2013.

Yet there is no guarantee that today's young women will sustain their near parity with men in earnings in the years to come. Recent cohorts of young women have fallen further behind their same-aged male counterparts as they have aged and dealt with the responsibilities of parenthood and family. For women, marriage and motherhood are both associated with less time spent on paid work-related activities. For men, the onset of family responsibilities has a reverse effect on their career.

The new Pew Research survey finds that among working parents of all ages with children younger than 18, mothers are three times as likely as fathers to say that being a working parent has made it harder for them to advance in their job or career (51% vs. 16%).

The survey also finds that women are much more likely than men to experience family-related career interruptions. Among mothers who have ever worked, 39% say they have taken a significant amount of time off from work to care for a child or family member. This compares with only 24% of working fathers.

Women who have experienced a significant career interruption in order to care for a family member have few regrets. They overwhelmingly say they are glad they did this, even though a significant share say it hurt their career overall.

For their part, young women today who have not yet had children expect that when they do, the impact on their careers will be negative. Among those ages 18 to 32, 63% think that having children will make it harder for them to advance in their job or career.

Gender, Work and Wages

In 2012, the median hourly wage for women, full-time and part-time workers combined, was 84% as much as men ($14.90 vs. $17.79). In 1980, the gap had been much wider: The median hourly wage for women was 64% as much as men ($11.94 vs. $18.57 per hour, in 2012 dollars).

The narrowing of the gap can be attributed mainly to the rising earnings of women. Armed with more education, greater labor force participation and an increased presence in more lucrative occupations, women have seen their median hourly wages rise by 25% over the past 30 years.

But losses for men—particularly young men—have also contributed to the narrowing wage gap. Overall, the median hourly wage for men decreased 4% from 1980–2012. The decline has been much sharper among young men (20%), contributing to the dramatic narrowing of the wage gap between young men and young women.

Overall, women account for nearly half of the U.S. labor force today—47% in 2012, up from 43% in 1980. This trend is a result of the increase in their labor force participation rate, from 52% in 1980 to 58% in 2012. Among young women (ages 25 to 34), 74% were in the labor force in 2012, up from 66% in 1980. Labor force participation among men has declined significantly over the past 30 years, from 78% in 1980 to 70% in 2012. Each new wave of young adult men (younger than 35) has been less active in the labor market than the preceding wave.

The employment and wage gains made by young women in recent decades are undoubtedly linked to the gains they have made in educational attainment. Among older millennials today (those ages 25 to 32), 38% of women have a bachelor's degree, compared with 31% of men. And among younger millennials (those ages 18 to 24), women are more likely than men to be enrolled in college (45% vs. 38% in 2012). These educational gaps in favor of women emerged in the 1990s and have widened since then.

As women have outpaced men in college education, their share of employment in the most skilled category of workers has risen sharply. In 2012, 49% of employed workers with at least a bachelor's degree were women, up from 36% in 1980. And women have made inroads into higher-skilled, higher-paying occupations. Still, notable gaps remain in the type of work done by women and men, and research indicates that women remain concentrated in female-dominated lesser-paying occupations and that integration slowed over the past decade.

Clearly, millennial women are well situated for career success and advancement. However, analysis going back to 1980 suggests that the gender gap in earnings may increase for them as it has for earlier cohorts of young women. Looking at the most recent cohorts of young women, by the time they reached their mid-30s, their earnings relative to those of men began to fall further behind, even if they had started out ahead of the previous cohort of young women. Motherhood is one factor, as it can lead to interruptions in career paths for women and increased time spent on unpaid work at home.

Most millennial women aren't there yet, but when they do have young children at home, their level of participation in the labor force is likely to decline.

There has been much scholarly research about the under-lying causes of the gender wage gap. Most, but not all, of the wage gap can be explained by certain measurable factors such as educational attainment, occupational segregation and dif-ferences in the number of hours worked (even among full-time workers). But there are other forces at work that are dif-ficult to quantify: gender stereotypes, discrimination, professional networks that are more robust for men than for women, and hesitancy on the part of women to aggressively negotiate for raises and promotions. Experts suggest that these factors may account for anywhere from 20% to 40% of the earnings gap.

Data on earnings, education and occupation do not pro-vide insight into these unmeasured factors. However, data from the new Pew Research survey helps to illuminate the at-titudes and experiences of men and women and give insight into how they navigate the workplace in an era of a narrow-ing, yet persistent, gender gap in pay.

Most Women Say the Playing Field Is Not Level . . .

The overall trends that are revealed in the economic data are reflected in public attitudes about gender and work. Ameri-cans see less gender-based inequality today than they did 20 to 30 years ago. At the same time, a large majority says this

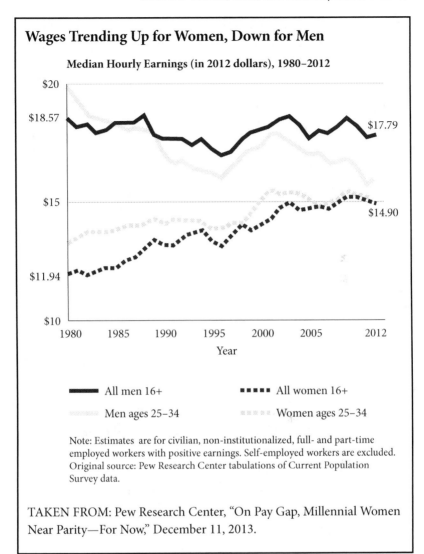

Wages Trending Up for Women, Down for Men

Median Hourly Earnings (in 2012 dollars), 1980–2012

— All men 16+   ▪▪▪▪▪ All women 16+

⋯⋯ Men ages 25–34   ⋇ ⋇ ⋇ Women ages 25–34

Note: Estimates are for civilian, non-institutionalized, full- and part-time employed workers with positive earnings. Self-employed workers are excluded. Original source: Pew Research Center tabulations of Current Population Survey data.

TAKEN FROM: Pew Research Center, "On Pay Gap, Millennial Women Near Parity—For Now," December 11, 2013.

country needs to continue making changes to give men and women equality in the workplace.

Significant gender differences are evident on these measures—with women much more likely than men to say that the two genders are not treated equally. Women are united in their views across generations: Millennial women, who are starting their careers on fairly equal footing with their male counterparts, are just as likely as older generations to believe that women face an uphill climb in terms of being treated equally by society and by employers.

Overall, the public is divided on the question of how society treats men and women. Many more say society generally favors men over women (45%) than say society favors women over men (9%). Four in ten adults say society generally treats men and women equally. Attitudes have shifted significantly over the past two decades. When the Gallup organization asked a similar question in 1993, a solid majority of adults (62%) said society favored men over women.

Women are much more likely than men to say society favors men (53% vs. 36%). Women are also more likely to say that society needs to do more to ensure equality in the workplace (72% vs. 61% of men). The gender gap on this question is particularly wide among millennials: 75% of millennial women compared with 57% of millennial men say the country needs to do more in order to bring about workplace equality.

The strong sense among the public that more change is needed may be related to the perception among many that there are gender-based disparities in wages and in hiring. Fully 55% of the public says if a man and a woman are doing the same work, the man generally earns more. And 46% of adults say it is easier for men to get top executive jobs in business and government than it is for women (43% say gender does not make a difference in this regard).

The gender pattern persists on these questions, with women much more likely than men to see built-in advantages for men in the workplace. In addition there is a significant education gap. College-educated adults are much more likely than those without a college degree to say that men generally out-earn women and that it's easier for men to get top-level jobs. Among women with a bachelor's degree or higher—the women most likely to be competing with men for top jobs—

fully 71% say it's easier for men to get these jobs than it is for women. Only 47% of women without a bachelor's degree agree.

. . . Yet Few See Unfair Conditions at Their Own Workplace

While there is a general perception, especially among women, that men have an unfair advantage when it comes to wages and hiring, relatively few working adults report these types of gender biases at their own workplace. Large majorities of working men (73%) and working women (75%) say that where they work, men and women are paid about the same amount for doing the same job. Only about one in ten says women are paid less than men.

Similar majorities of men (73%) and women (72%) say that at their workplace, women have about the same opportunities as men to advance to top executive and professional positions. Some 14% say women have fewer opportunities for promotions or advancement.

Overall, one in seven adults (14%) who have ever worked say they have been the victim of gender discrimination on the job. A higher share of women (18%) than men (10%) report having experienced this type of discrimination.

For those women who say they have been discriminated against because of their gender, about half say this had a negative impact on their career. For this relatively small minority of women (10% of all women with experience in the labor force), the negative consequences have been significant: The vast majority say the discrimination had a "big" impact on their career.

Gender, Work and Leaning In

In recent decades, women have clearly expanded their footprint in the managerial ranks of corporate America. According to data from the U.S. Bureau of Labor Statistics, in 1980, only

7% of women were working in managerial and administrative occupations, compared with 17% of men. This gap has all but disappeared: 15% of women were in these occupations in 2012, compared with 17% of men. Still, women have yet to come anywhere close to parity with men in the upper echelon of corporate America. According to the nonprofit research group Catalyst, women currently hold 4.2% of Fortune 500 CEO [chief executive officer] positions and 4.5% of Fortune 1000 CEO positions.

In the new Pew Research survey, respondents were asked to assess the level of focus men and women bring to their careers. Across age groups, majorities say that the men and women they know who are around their age are about equally focused on their careers. Among those who see a clear difference in focus between men and women, millennials are the only ones who say women are more focused on their careers than men.

Even so, the survey finds that women are less likely than men to say they have asked for a raise or promotion and less likely to say that they would like to be a boss or senior manager someday. Overall, 47% of adults with at least some work experience say they have asked for a pay raise or promotion at some point in their working life: 51% of men have done so, as have 43% of women. Among millennials, 48% of men and 42% of women, a statistically insignificant difference, say they have asked for a pay raise or promotion. However, there is a wide gender gap among Gen Xers [those born during the late 1960s and 1970s]: 59% of Gen X men, compared with 47% of Gen X women, say they've sought to advance their career in this way.

Six in ten men (excluding those who are retired) say they either would like to be the boss at their workplace or they already are the boss. This compares with 44% of women. Some 53% of women say they don't have any interest in being the boss. These attitudes are shaped in part by where people are in the life cycle. Young adults are more likely than middle-aged and older adults to say they'd like to be the boss some-day—possibly because they have more time ahead of them to reach that goal.

Among those who are not already the boss or a top manager at their workplace, millennial men are somewhat more likely than millennial women to say they'd like to be the boss. However, a significant gender gap opens up among Gen Xers and boomers [referring to baby boomers, those born between 1946 and 1964]. Among Gen Xers, 58% of men, compared with 41% of women, say they would like to be the boss some-day. Gen X women are among the most likely to have children under the age of 18, and this may well be a factor in views about how much additional responsibility they would want to take on at work.

The Balancing Act

As the economic data suggest, the focus and intensity that many young women bring to their careers can diminish as they age and take on more responsibility outside of the work-place. The survey findings illustrate some of the specific challenges women face in accommodating the demands of work and family. Among working women with children under age 18, fully half (51%) say being a working parent has made it harder for them to advance in their job or career. By compari-son, only 16% of men with children under age 18 say being a working parent has made it harder for them to advance at work.

When young adults who do not yet have children consider that possibility, most see roadblocks ahead. Fully 62% of child-less millennials expect that having children will make it harder for them to advance in their career. Roughly one-third (34%) say having children won't make a difference in their career ad-vancement, and only 1% say having children is likely to help them advance. There is no gender gap on this question among young adults. Millennial men and women tend to agree that having children will make it harder for them to advance at work.

> *"It's the structural barriers to women's progress and enduring social attitudes about women's place that contribute the most to women's lower pay, according to economic analyses of the wage gap."*

The Gender Wage Gap Is Caused by a Variety of Factors

Sarah Jane Glynn

In the following viewpoint, Sarah Jane Glynn argues that much confusion surrounds the wage gap and the commonly cited 77-cent statistic. Glynn contends that it is true that women and men tend to work in different occupations, have different levels of education and experience, and make different choices about work. Nonetheless, Glynn claims that even when all of these factors are taken into account, the gender wage gap cannot be fully explained without positing some level of discrimination. Glynn is director for women's economic policy at the Center for American Progress.

Sarah Jane Glynn, "Explaining the Gender Wage Gap," Center for American Progress, May 19, 2014, pp. 1–6. Copyright © 2014 Center for American Progress. All rights reserved. Reproduced with permission.

As you read, consider the following questions:

1. How is the 77-cent statistic calculated, according to Glynn?

2. According to Glynn, women work approximately how much less per day than men?

3. The author claims that according to research by two Cornell University economists, approximately what fraction of the wage gap is not related to occupation, education, and years of experience?

The most commonly cited statistic for the gender wage gap asserts that women earn only 77 cents for every dollar earned by men. However, a great deal of contention surrounds statistics measuring and quantifying the gender wage gap, and this confusion is not entirely without merit. Some of the controversy around wage-gap estimates and figures is at least partly due to the fact that, like many statistics, the exact figure changes slightly depending on the data source used. With competing statistics and a highly politicized issue, the very existence of the wage gap is often called into question—along with its significance and driving causes.

Confusion About the Wage Gap

The "77 cents" formulation is a colloquialism—shorthand for expressing a complex economic truth. Simply put, what it conveys is the fact that, if you average out what all women, working full-time, year-round, earn and compare that number to what all men working full-time, year-round, earn, you find that women take home 77 percent of what men do.

The confusion around wage-gap calculations is further fueled when people misspeak about the nature of the number, what it reflects, and to which groups of workers it refers. To be very clear, the 77-cents-on-the-dollar statistic does not compare men and women doing identical work. This has led

to critics charging that the 77-cent figure is a willful manipulation of truth that does not accurately reflect gender discrimination in the workplace. In reality, the 77-cent figure
does capture some discrimination, but it also reflects gender
differences in jobs, hours worked, years of experience, educational attainment, or personal choices that people make about
their careers. Incorporating these significant factors is precisely what makes the number valuable.

This [viewpoint] explains how the wage gap is calculated,
why the numbers are not all the same, and what causes are
driving the most commonly cited 77-cent figure.

The 77-Cent Figure

Like all statistics, the 77-cent statistic tells a particular story.
It's calculated by dividing the median earnings of full-time,
year-round, working women by the median earnings of full-
time, year-round, working men, all rounded to the nearest
$100.

The wage gap looks slightly different depending on which
data source is used in the calculation. Outcomes look margin-
ally different, for example, depending on whether weekly or
annual earnings are compared. Annual data for 2012, the latest year for which data are available, estimate that women
earn 77 percent of what men do for working full-time, year-
round, while weekly data put the estimate at 82.1 percent. But
this is not an issue unique to calculating the gender wage gap,
since most statistics vary slightly when pulling data from different sources using different measures of analysis. Similarly,
the estimate of the median annual wage for all full-time workers regardless of gender—$45,535 in 2012—is not the same as
the median weekly wage for all full-time workers—$765 to
$772 depending on the quarter—multiplied by 52.

The annual wage-gap statistic average is compiled by
grouping together many people—and, as such, it has its cave-
ats. In real life, men and women often do not hold the same

jobs. Neither do they, on average, have the same years of experience, work the same hours, or equally share the responsibility of childbirth and child care. All of these factors translate, to different degrees, into lower pay.

And it's all of these factors coming together—in the same way that they do in real life—that gives the 77-cent comparison meaning. The varied factors that influence the wage gap—different jobs, different hours, and different work histories—are not purely the result of women's choices. There are significant structural factors that influence the decisions working women make that result in lower pay, and these deserve as much attention as overt discrimination.

Occupational Differences

One of the largest driving factors of the gender wage gap is the fact that men and women, on average, work in different industries and occupations; this accounts for up to 49.3 percent of the wage gap, according to some estimates. Women are much more likely than men to be clustered in just a few occupations, with nearly half of all working women—44.4 percent—employed in just 20 occupations, including secretaries and administrative assistants, registered nurses, and school teachers. Meanwhile, only about one-third—34.8 percent—of men are employed in the top 20 occupations for male workers, including truck drivers, managers, and supervisors.

Interestingly, only four occupations—retail salespersons, first-line supervisors and managers of retail stores, cooks, and all other managers—appear in both genders' top 20 most common occupations. Not only are women more likely to be concentrated in fewer types of jobs, those jobs are more likely to be female dominated—a fact that often leads to lower wages. Female-dominated industries pay lower wages than male-dominated industries requiring similar skill levels, and the effect is stronger in jobs that require higher levels of education. Women are more likely to be concentrated in low-wage work, and they make up the majority of minimum-wage workers in the United States. The top 10 occupations for women all pay men more on average, including secretaries and administrative assistants, registered nurses, teachers, and cashiers. In fact, out of the 534 occupations tracked by the Bureau of Labor Statistics, only seven pay women more than men on average, such as respiratory therapists and stock clerks. The jobs that pay women more on average employ about 1.5 million women, or approximately 3 percent of the full-time female labor force.

The highest wage premium for women is among respiratory therapists, an occupation where women earn 6.4 percent more than men—the equivalent of an extra $62 per week. That is certainly nothing to scoff at, but it pales in comparison to the occupations with the worst wage gap for women: property, real estate, and community association managers. In these jobs, women earn, on average, 60.6 percent of what men do within the same occupation—the equivalent of losing an astonishing $473 dollars per week. Put another way, the wage losses per week of women property managers is about equal to the wage premium that women respiratory therapists earn over two months.

So while the 77-cent figure compares working women and men in different jobs, it is influenced by occupational segregation and the different wages men and women earn even within the same types of jobs.

All this could be used to argue that the wages for men and women would be the same if only women were not choosing traditionally female-dominated industries. But in reality, there are several factors that lead women to traditionally female-dominated roles, including the gendered socialization that trains girls from childhood to embody the sorts of traits that translate well into traditionally feminine jobs centered on nurturing, service, and supporting other people in their jobs. As the following sections illustrate, there are structural factors that influence the different career paths of men and women—factors that should be addressed to ensure that all workers are able to work and contribute to the economy in ways that make the most of their abilities and strengths.

Differences in Hours

Women not only work in different occupations, but they also work fewer hours in the workplace: 35 minutes less per day than men, among full-time working men and women. What accounts for that difference in time? Interestingly, when home and child care work is taken into account, the time gap looks very different. Employed mothers with a child under age 6 spend about 47 more minutes per day caring for and helping household members, compared to employed fathers. Parents of older children also have a caring time gap, though it is smaller—about 22 minutes per day. The data suggest that women's reduction in work hours can be accounted for when taking into consideration the fact that women provide more unpaid care in the home, at least in homes with children.

While the fact that full-time working women put in fewer hours on average certainly affects the wage gap, the penalty women pay for working less is not as straightforward as a simple subtraction in hourly wages. Harvard economist Claudia Goldin has found that in some well-paid occupations, such as business and law, people who work very long hours receive a disproportionate increase in their wages—which means that those who work fewer hours receive disproportionately lower pay. In these types of jobs, for example, working 20 percent fewer hours results in a reduction in compensation of more than 20 percent. Some research shows that the career costs of childbearing are particularly high for highly skilled women in professional occupations, likely in part because there is not a direct relationship between hours and wages for women who find themselves on the "mommy track."

Some critics use this as fuel for their argument that the wage gap only exists because women scale back their work hours to care for their families. But that belief rests upon a very abstract take on reality. The fact is, in real life, women work the way they do for reasons that, for all but the most privileged, have very little to do with choosing purely between work and family life. In fact, there is a cyclical relationship between women's wages and unpaid care work within the home.

Family Caregiving

When women earn less to begin with, often due to occupational segregation, it may make economic sense for them to be the ones to scale back to provide family care for children or aging relatives. In turn, that reduction in job hours and job tenure both lowers women's wages overall and contributes to the cultural notion that women are not as devoted to employment once they have children. Mothers, on average, have lower earnings than women without children, and while some of this gap may be due to working fewer hours, at least some of it persists even when productivity is taken into account. The unfortunate truth is that mothers are perceived as less dedicated employees after having children because many employers think mothers will be distracted by their home lives. At the same time, men tend to receive pay increases after becoming fathers, in part because fathers are assumed to be the breadwinners for their families even though most married men have working partners.

There's also the fact that women are now more likely than ever before to be raising children without a partner—carrying all the weight of breadwinning and homemaking on their own shoulders. Nearly two-thirds of mothers are the primary or co-breadwinners for their families. And this does not even begin to take into account the lack of federal laws in this country that could help manage conflicts between caring for a family while still bringing in income.

There is currently no mandate in the United States that ensures workers have access to paid sick days, and as a result, roughly 40 percent of workers risk losing a day's pay or their jobs if they or a family member fall ill. Mothers are more likely than fathers to stay home with sick children, and one-third of parents of young children report that they are concerned about losing their jobs or their wages if they have to stay home with an ill child, according to the C.S. Mott Children's Hospital National Poll on Children's Health.

The United States is one of only a few countries in the world, and certainly the only advanced economy, where mothers do not have the right to paid maternity leave after the birth of a new child. Currently, only 12 percent of workers have access to paid family leave, and when mothers have to take unpaid time out of the labor force, it results in longer gaps in work histories with a negative impact on future wages, compared to mothers who have access to paid leave. Because so few women have access to paid maternity leave, and because the biological realities of childbirth mean that most women have no choice but to take time off after having children, mothers end up spending more time out of the labor force than fathers, which further contributes to the gender wage gap.

"Unexplained" Drivers of the Wage Gap

Cornell economists Francine D. Blau and Lawrence M. Kahn have managed to quantify what percentage of the pay gap between men and women is due to aspects we cannot easily measure—aspects that go beyond things such as occupation, educational attainment, and years of experience. According to Blau and Kahn, this percentage is 41.1 percent. At least some of this is due to discrimination, even if it is subtle and subconscious. Combating gender and caregiver pay discrimination is a real and important challenge facing our country, which is why laws such as the Equal Pay Act of 1963 and the Lilly Ledbetter Fair Pay Act of 2009 are so important.

But the rest of the wage gap—nearly 60 percent—is influenced by all the structural and social factors that drive the decisions women make about where and how long they work. These factors constrain the choices that lead them to work and earn less. Altogether, they are why the 77-cent figure is meaningful: Comparing a woman and a man in the same occupation and with the same background in a very narrow way only tells you one part of the story—even though a gender wage gap still persists within these types of comparisons.

The good news is that some of these issues can be addressed through public policy. The Healthy Families Act would ensure that workers have access to paid sick days and would no longer have to worry about taking a financial hit if they or their children were to fall ill. The Family and Medical Insurance Leave Act, or FAMILY Act, would create a federal paid family and medical leave program that would provide up to 12 weeks of partial wage replacement after the birth of a new child, to provide care to a seriously ill family member, or to recover from a worker's own serious illness, building on the job protection offered by the Family and Medical Leave Act of 1993.

It's the structural barriers to women's progress and enduring social attitudes about women's place that contribute the most to women's lower pay, according to economic analyses of the wage gap. Understanding these constraints and what causes the gender wage gap is an important first step to change structural barriers.

> *"Any wage gap is rooted more in social trends and tendencies than malicious discrimination by employers."*

The Gender Wage Gap Is Due to Women's Choices

June E. O'Neill

In the following viewpoint, June E. O'Neill argues that there is no gender wage gap that applies to all women and men of all ages. Any difference in wages of men and women, O'Neill claims, can be explained by education, experience, and personal choices. The author contends that there is no evidence of rampant gender discrimination and no need for new legislation to protect women. O'Neill is the Wollman Distinguished Professor of Economics and the director of the Center for the Study of Business and Government at the Zicklin School of Business at Baruch College.

As you read, consider the following questions:

1. Among what group of men and women does the wage gap against women turn into a wage premium, according to the author?

2. Why do women tend to work in the fields that are dominated by women, according to O'Neill?

3. According to O'Neill, what two existing pieces of legislation are sufficient to check discrimination in the workplace?

A single, oft-cited statistic is that women make 79 cents for every dollar that men make doing the same work. However, that average number fails to account for factors aside from discrimination that can affect an individual's pay. When experience and other factors are considered, the wage gap narrows.

Comparing single childless women to single childless men, ages 35–43, the wage gap not only disappears, but instead becomes a wage premium. Nevertheless, Americans are likely to hear much about the much-exaggerated wage gap during the election campaign.

Education and Experience

The National Longitudinal Survey of Youth (NLSY) administered to 11,406 civilian students in 1979 who were reinterviewed in subsequent years, offers a more precise understanding of the gender pay gap. Follow-ups to the original survey in 2000 (when participants were ages 35–43) and in 2008 (when they were ages 43–51) show that a number of factors influence male and female hourly wages. Employer discrimination is not an important reason for the apparent wage gap.

The Armed Forces Qualification Test (AFQT) was administered to nearly all survey participants and serves as a proxy for basic cognitive skills contributing to occupation productivity. Combined with results from the NLSY measuring the level of schooling completed, these two factors explain approximately one-half of a cent of the wage gap, decreasing it from 79.0 cents to 79.4 cents on the dollar.

An Insulting Explanation for the Gender Wage Gap

Activist groups like the National Organization for Women have a fallback position: that women's education and career choices are not truly free—they are driven by powerful sexist stereotypes. . . .

Here is the problem: American women are among the best informed and most self-determining human beings in the world. To say that they are manipulated into their life choices by forces beyond their control is divorced from reality and demeaning.

Christina Hoff Sommers,
"5 Feminist Myths That Will Not Die,"
Time, *September 2, 2014.*

Accounting for the fact that men tend to have better-developed occupational histories markedly reduces the gender wage gap:

- In 2000, the average woman surveyed had about two years less work experience than the average man in military and civilian jobs combined.

- Moreover, close to 14 percent of the weeks worked by women were part-time compared to 5 percent for men.

- When this variation in work experience is applied to 2008 wage data, the gender wage gap closes from 79.4 cents to 88.6 cents on the dollar.

The Impact of Personal Choices

Because child-rearing and other family responsibilities fall disproportionately upon women, they are significantly more likely to leave the workforce for an extended period. Furthermore, women are more likely to seek employment at nonprofits or in government agencies—employment which is associated with lower pay. These positions are usually more flexible and amenable to the needs of working mothers. Accounting for this difference, the wage gap further shrinks from 88.6 cents to 90.9 cents.

Women tend to work in fields dominated by women, in large part because these fields best satisfy women's dual careers as workers and household managers. This can include less stressful work environments (noise, strenuous activity, etc.), more flexible policies regarding time off, and a number of other factors. The inclusion of this variable further closes the wage gap from 90.9 cents to 96.7 cents.

Thus, of the 21-cent differential, 17.7 cents, or 84.3 percent of the total wage gap, can be explained by largely innocuous, non-discriminatory factors that have more to do with career and life choices than employers' prejudices. Thus, the charge of wage discrimination based on the 77-cent statistic is grossly misleading.

In fact, the unadjusted average hourly wage in 2000 of single women who have never had a child was 7.9 percent greater than that of their male counterparts. This comparison implies that any wage gap is rooted more in social trends and tendencies than malicious discrimination by employers. It undermines the justification for government intervention to eliminate the wage gap.

An Issue Based on Myth

Advocates of the federal Paycheck Fairness Act claim that passage of the bill is a crucial step in gaining pay equity for women. The act would require employers to justify pay differentials between men and women with similar job titles by requiring employers to prove that a standard qualification such as relevant work experience is a job-related necessity. Employees would also be empowered to propose alternative methods for setting pay more to their liking. Endless lawsuits would be further encouraged by provisions that fatten damages and make it easier to bring class-action suits. Yet existing legislation including the Equal Pay Act of 1963 and the Civil Rights Act of 1964 and its amendments are surely sufficient to check discrimination.

The act is unlikely to be voted on during this session of Congress. Democrats failed to get the 60-vote majority needed in the Senate to bring the bill up for a vote, and the House of Representatives is controlled by Republicans, who oppose the bill. However, gender pay discrimination is likely to be an election issue, even though it is based on a myth.

> *"When economists examine the gap and control for all measurable factors, there remains a residual portion they can't explain."*

The Gender Wage Gap Is Ugly. So Is the Right-Wing Effort to Deny It

Bryce Covert

In the following viewpoint, Bryce Covert argues that efforts to explain away the gender wage gap are misguided. Covert contends that the wage gap is real and women do make less money than men. Furthermore, she claims that although there are valid disagreements about the various causes of the gap, research supports discrimination against women as a significant cause of the gender wage gap. She suggests that increased workplace flexibility and legislation could help eliminate some of this discrimination. Covert is the economic policy editor for ThinkProgress *and a contributor for the* Nation.

As you read, consider the following questions:

1. According to Covert, economist Claudia Goldin found that the wage gap differs over a woman's lifetime for what main reason?

2. Women make up what fraction of the country's minimum wage workers, according to Covert?

3. According to the author, what happens to the gender wage gap in workplaces where information on salaries is widely available?

Conservatives were not at all happy when President Obama issued executive orders to close the gender pay gap earlier this month. And they were particularly angry that Obama justified the change by arguing, famously, "[T]he average full-time working woman earns just 77 cents for every dollar a man earns."

The figure, according to conservatives, is bunk. And to make their point, they cited an unpredictable source: Claudia Goldin, a highly respected Harvard economist whose research on inequalities facing women in the economy has been widely cited by feminist causes. Here, for example, was Kay Hymowitz, from the right-leaning Manhattan Institute, during an appearance on MSNBC's *All In with Chris Hayes*:

> . . . we hear all the time, we just heard from the president recently that women only make 77 cents on the dollar. Well, those are raw numbers. Its gross averages that don't take into account hours worked. They don't take into account professions and occupations. And when you take all that into account and time offing [sic] for having children, absolutely—then the numbers look very similar. And there's a recent paper that was just released by Claudia Goldin at Harvard basically saying, yes, we have achieved a kind of parity.

But while Goldin's research says many things, it doesn't say the wage gap is phony. Just ask Goldin herself.

In her research, Goldin found that the wage gap differs over a woman's lifetime and increases with age. And the biggest reason is a lack of flexibility when it comes to working hours. "The gender gap in pay would be considerably reduced and might even vanish if firms did not have an incentive to disproportionately reward individuals who worked long hours and who worked particular hours," Goldin writes. If firms could offer workers more options for how much to work and when to work, she thinks, the wage gap between men and women who work the same hours would nearly disappear.

So what does Goldin think of the 77 cents figure? I asked her. "It's an accurate statement of what it is," she said. She compared it to a thermometer: It gives you a reading of the temperature, although it won't tell you if the weather is going to change or if it's an abnormal day. In the same way, 77 cents does in fact measure the difference in earnings between all men and women who work full-time, year-round at the median, although it doesn't reveal all the relevant information— and might obscure some very important details.

There's room for honest disagreement over the precise role that different factors play in causing the gender gap. But, Goldin says, discrimination is clearly part of the story. "There's no question that there is" discrimination, she said. "We see incredible evidence of it in court cases that reach the front pages." One such case made news just last month, when 16 women filed a class-action lawsuit against Sterling Jewelers, which owns Jared and Kay. The suit alleges, among other things, that women were routinely paid less than similar or less qualified men and denied promotions that would have increased their pay. (The suit also alleges severe instances of sexual harassment, some perpetrated on the very women being paid less.)

One-Third of the Pay Gap
Is Unexplained

Although education and employment factors explain a substantial part of the pay gap, they do not explain it in its entirety. Regression analysis allows us to analyze the effect of multiple factors on earnings at the same time. One might expect that when you compare men and women with the same major, who attended the same type of institution and worked the same hours in the same job in the same economic sector, the pay gap would disappear. But this is not what our analysis shows. Our regression analysis finds that just over one-third of the pay gap cannot be explained by any of these factors and appears to be attributable to gender alone. That is, after we controlled for all the factors included in our analysis that we found to affect earnings, college-educated women working full-time earned an unexplained 7 percent less than their male peers did one year out of college.

Christianne Corbett and Catherine Hill,
"Graduating to a Pay Gap," American Association
of University Women (AAUW), October 2012.

There's also research that points to discrimination as a factor in that 23 percent difference between men's and women's earnings. When economists examine the gap and control for all measurable factors, there remains a residual portion they can't explain. For the Government Accountability Office, that portion was 20 percent. For economists Francine Blau and Lawrence Kahn, it was 41 percent. It's in this unexplainable portion where discrimination may be leaving its mark.

One other reason conservative analysts are misusing Goldin's paper is that they miss one of its key nuances: Her research focused on a particular subset of people, not the entire country. "It specifically says that I'm only looking at . . . individuals with incomes greater than $60,000 a year," she told me. Part of this is because she has found that "the gender gap is larger in high-income jobs," she said, "and the gender gap within jobs is phenomenally more important" than the differences between men and women who work in different jobs.

But the gender gap in lower-paying jobs is still very real. Maids make $19,570 a year at the median, for example, while janitors make $22,590. Generally speaking, low-skill jobs that are 75 percent or more female pay nearly $150 less a week than those dominated by men. It's worse for high-skill jobs, where women's fields pay $471 less. On the other hand, men make more when they buck societal expectations and take jobs in these areas. Women are also nearly two-thirds of the country's minimum wage workers. All of these factors contribute to an earnings gap, and they aren't all about women's choices. They're about how society values work when women do it and what kind of jobs are available to them.

Goldin's emphasis on the relationship between more flexible working hours and lower wage gaps can fix the gap at the hourly level. It would allow women who put in the same hours as men—no matter when they put them in—to earn the same rate. Of course, flexibility probably wouldn't have a big impact on the annual wage gap, which reflects the fact that women are much more likely than men to have to interrupt or completely pause their careers to care for children. "You work less, you get less," she noted. But that doesn't mean the government is powerless to reduce the annual wage gap. Initiatives like affordable child care and paid family leave can make it easier for caregivers—who, even now, are predominantly women—to pick up the kids from school or take time off for a new baby. It might also encourage more men to do the same things. "There's no question that they're complementary," she said.

As for the solutions that President Obama and Democrats have suggested, there's no reason they can't coexist with Goldin's findings. Obama's executive order is aimed at increasing wage transparency, as is the Paycheck Fairness Act. And the wage gaps are smaller—and shrinking—in places where information on salaries is widely available, like the federal government or unionized jobs. Simply giving women more information about their pay so that they can address discrimination if and when it does happen is one small piece of the gender wage gap puzzle.

> "For a very large segment of the black
> population, not only that bottom 20%,
> their relative position has gotten some-
> what worse."

Black-White Income
Differences: What's Happened?

Arthur MacEwan

*In the following viewpoint, Arthur MacEwan argues that despite
talk of the United States as a post-racial society since the election
of President Barack Obama, income inequality between black
households and white households has not decreased by much in
the past forty years. MacEwan claims that wealthy black households have done very well in the last few decades, but the rest of
black households have fared poorly economically compared to
similarly situated white households. MacEwan is professor emeri-
tus of economics at the University of Massachusetts Boston.*

As you read, consider the following questions:

1. According to the author, in 2011 the median income of
   black households was what percentage of the median
   income of white households?

2. What was the average income of the bottom 20 percent of black households in 2011, according to MacEwan?

3. How many times greater was the net worth of white households than black households in 2009, according to the author?

With a president who is African American and talk of a "post-racial" society, one might think that the economic position of African Americans relative to European Americans had improved significantly over the last 40 or so years. One would be wrong.

In 2011, the median income of black households was about $32,000; that is, half of black households had income above this figure, and half had incomes below this figure. This was 61.7% of the 2011 median income of white households. In 1970, before the general increase of income inequality, the figure was 60.9%, just a smidgen lower. Not much change. Also, there has been virtually no change if mean incomes are used for the black-white comparison. (The "mean" is the average—the total income of all households in the group divided by the number of households.)

This lack of change over the last 40 years might come as a surprise, contrary to visible indicators of improvement in the position of black people. We see, for example, many black professionals in fields where 40 years ago there were few. There are also more black executives—even a few CEOs of major corporations. And there is Barack Obama. How do these visible changes square with the lack of change in the relative income positions of blacks and whites?

The answer to this question is largely that the distribution of income among black households is very unequal, even more unequal than the distribution of income among white households. So many of the prominent black people who appear to be doing so well are indeed doing well. At the other end are the black households that are doing worse. Between

1970 and 2011, the upper 5% of black households saw their average (mean) incomes rise from about $114,000 to about $215,000 (measured in 2011 dollars), while the incomes of black households in the bottom 20% saw their average income fall from $6,465 to $6,379.

Among white households, the pattern of change was similar but not quite so extreme. The average income of the top 5% of white households rose by 83% in this period, as compared to the 88% increase for the top black households—though that elite white group was still taking in 50% per household more than their black counterparts. The bottom 20% of white households saw a 13% increase per household in their inflation-adjusted incomes between 1970 and 2011.

So high-income blacks have done pretty well—even slightly improved relative to the top white households. They have to a degree benefited from the social changes of recent decades. But for a very large segment of the black population, not only that bottom 20%, their relative position has gotten somewhat worse, and for many their absolute incomes have actually fallen. The long-term reduction of the minimum wage (in real terms) has had an especially harsh impact on low-income blacks, and the weakening of labor unions has also harmed a broad swath of the black community. Add the mass incarceration of young black men and their consequent exclusion from the economic mainstream, and it is not hard to understand continuing black-white inequality.

Two other points should be kept in mind: First, the changes between 1970 and 2011 have not been smooth. Measured by either the mean or the median, the income position of black households relative to white households was fairly stable in the 1970s, fell off sharply in the early 1980s, and rose again to a peak in the late 1990s before falling off to its current level.

Second, income distribution is only one measure of economic inequality. The Great Recession had a devastating impact on the wealth of black households, largely explained by the impact of the housing crisis. In 2004, the net worth of white households was about eleven times that of black households (bad enough), about the same as it had been since the early 1980s (with a slight improvement in the mid-1990s). But by 2009, though both black and white net worth fell from 2004, white net worth was 19 times black net worth.

The more things change, the more they stay the same—or get worse!

> "The racial wealth gap is three times
> larger than the racial income gap."

Racial Disparities in Wealth Are Even Worse than Income Inequality

Signe-Mary McKernan, Caroline Ratcliffe, Eugene Steuerle, and Sisi Zhang

In the following viewpoint, Signe-Mary McKernan, Caroline Ratcliffe, Eugene Steuerle, and Sisi Zhang argue that although there is a racial income gap among black, Hispanic, and white households, there is an even larger gap in wealth. The authors contend that wealth inequality grows over time and keeps middle-income blacks and Hispanics from being able to weather tough times and build wealth. McKernan and Ratcliffe are senior fellows, Steuerle is an institute fellow, and Zhang is a research associate, all at the Urban Institute.

As you read, consider the following questions:

1. According to the authors, how much bigger (in dollars) was the average wealth of white families than black and Hispanic families in 2010?

Signe-Mary McKernan, Caroline Ratcliffe, Eugene Steuerle, and Sisi Zhang, "Less than Equal: Racial Disparities in Wealth Accumulation," Urban Institute, April 2013, pp. 1–5. www.urban.org. Reproduced by permission.

2. Hispanic families saw their wealth cut by what percentage between 2007 and 2010, according to the authors?

3. According to the authors, what are two key strategies that have an automatic component by which families build wealth?

Policy makers often focus on income and overlook wealth, but consider: the racial wealth gap is three times larger than the racial income gap. Such great wealth disparities help explain why many middle-income blacks and Hispanics haven't seen much improvement in their relative economic status and, in fact, are at greater risk of sliding backward.

Wealth Inequality and Income Inequality over Time

Wealth is not just for the wealthy. The poor can have wealth too—and that wealth can accrue over time or provide collateral for borrowing, giving families a way to move up and out of poverty. A home or a car can offer benefits far beyond its cash value. And even a small amount of savings can help families avoid falling into a vicious cycle of debt when a job loss or financial emergency hits.

Wealth disparities have worsened over the past 30 years. High-wealth families (the top 20 percent by net worth) saw their average wealth increase by nearly 120 percent between 1983 and 2010, while middle-wealth families saw their average wealth go up by only 13 percent. The lowest-wealth families—those in the bottom 20 percent—saw their average wealth fall well below zero, meaning their average debts exceed their assets.

There is extraordinary wealth inequality between the races. In 2010, whites on average had six times the wealth of blacks and Hispanics. So for every $6.00 whites had in wealth, blacks and Hispanics had $1.00 (or average wealth of $632,000 versus $103,000).

The income gap, by comparison, is much smaller. In 2010, the average income for whites was twice that of blacks and Hispanics ($89,000 versus $46,000), meaning that for every $2.00 whites earned, blacks and Hispanics earned $1.00.

How have these two measures changed over time? Neither has improved, but while the income gap has stayed roughly the same, the wealth gap has grown. In 1983, the average wealth of whites was roughly five times that of black and Hispanics.

In inflation-adjusted 2010 dollars, as opposed to ratios, the gap is also growing—as would happen in any growing economy if the ratios remained constant, much less moved farther apart. The average wealth of white families was $230,000 higher than the average wealth of black and Hispanic families in 1983. By 2010, the average wealth of white families was over a half-million dollars higher than the average wealth of black and Hispanic families ($632,000 versus $98,000 and $110,000, respectively). If we look at the median family, the wealth holdings are lower and the differences are smaller, but the trends are the same.

The Racial Wealth Gap over the Life Cycle

The racial wealth gap grows sharply with age. Early in wealth-building years (when adults are in their 30s), white families have 3.5 to 4 times the wealth of families of color. Over the life cycle, these initial racial differences grow in both absolute and relative terms.

Whites on average are on a higher accumulation curve than blacks or Hispanics. Whites age 32–40 in 1983 had an average family wealth of $184,000. In 2010, near their peak wealth-building years of age 59–67, average white family wealth had shot up to $1.1 million. In contrast, blacks age 32–40 in 1983 saw their average family wealth rise more slowly, from $54,000 to $161,000 by 2010. Meanwhile, average family wealth for Hispanics increased from $46,000 in 1983 to

$226,000 in 2010. In other words, whites in this cohort started with about three and a half times more wealth than blacks in their 30s but had seven times more wealth in their 60s. Compared with Hispanics, whites started with four times more wealth in their 30s but had nearly five times more wealth three decades later.

Blacks especially, but also Hispanics, are not on the same compound growth path. Particularly important, these families of color are less likely to own homes and have retirement accounts than whites, so they miss out on the automatic behavioral component of these traditionally powerful wealth-building vehicles. In 2010, fewer than half of black and Hispanic families owned homes, while three-quarters of white families did.

The Great Recession

While the Great Recession didn't cause the wealth disparities between whites and minorities, it did exacerbate them. The 2007–09 recession brought about sharp declines in the wealth of white, black, and Hispanic families alike, but Hispanics experienced the largest decline. Lower home values account for much of Hispanics' wealth loss, while retirement accounts are where blacks were hit hardest.

Between 2007 and 2010, Hispanic families saw their wealth cut by over 40 percent, and black families saw their wealth fall by 31 percent. By comparison, the wealth of white families fell by 11 percent.

Like a lot of young families, many Hispanic families bought homes just before the recession. Because they started with higher debt-to-asset values, the sharp decline in housing prices meant an even sharper cut in Hispanics' wealth. As a result, they were also more likely to end up underwater or with negative home equity. Between 2007 and 2010, Hispanics saw their home equity cut in half, compared with about a quarter for black and white families.

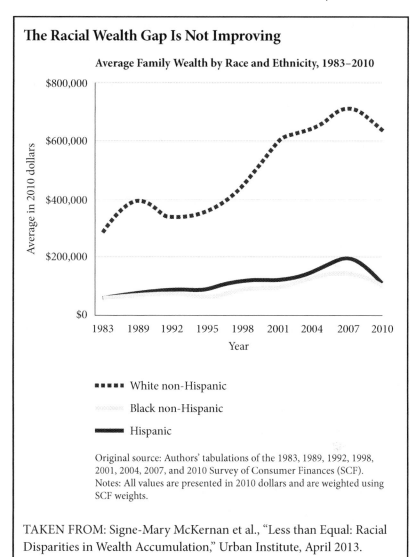

The Racial Wealth Gap Is Not Improving

Average Family Wealth by Race and Ethnicity, 1983–2010

■■■■■ White non-Hispanic

░░░░░ Black non-Hispanic

▬▬▬▬ Hispanic

Original source: Authors' tabulations of the 1983, 1989, 1992, 1998, 2001, 2004, 2007, and 2010 Survey of Consumer Finances (SCF). Notes: All values are presented in 2010 dollars and are weighted using SCF weights.

TAKEN FROM: Signe-Mary McKernan et al., "Less than Equal: Racial Disparities in Wealth Accumulation," Urban Institute, April 2013.

In contrast, black families lost the most in retirement assets, while white families experienced a slight increase. On average, blacks saw their retirement assets fall by 35 percent during the Great Recession, compared with a smaller (but still substantial) decline of 18 percent for Hispanic families. This finding is consistent with research that suggests lower-income families are more likely to withdraw money from retirement savings after a job loss or other adverse event. The high rates of unemployment and other financial needs that took hold with the Great Recession appear to have led to larger declines in retirement savings for black families.

The stock market has essentially recovered since the recession. So, those families able to hold onto their retirement saving over longer periods (such as those who remain employed or have other assets to which they can turn) come out much better than those who sell when markets are low.

The Solution

Families of color were disproportionately affected by the recession. However, the fact that they were not on good wealth-building paths before this financial crisis calls into question whether a whole range of policies (from tax to safety net) have actually been helping minorities get ahead in the modern economy. More fundamentally, it raises the question of whether social welfare policies pay too little attention to wealth building and mobility relative to consumption and income.

Because Hispanics and blacks are disproportionately low income, their wealth building is strongly affected by policies aimed at low-income families. Right now, safety net policies emphasize consumption: The Supplemental Nutrition Assistance Program and Temporary Assistance for Needy Families, for example, try to ensure that families have enough food to eat and other basic necessities. Many safety net programs even discourage saving: Families can become ineligible if they have a few thousand dollars in savings. Wealth-building policies, on the other hand, are delivered as tax subsidies for homeownership and retirement. Since families of color are less likely to be able to use these subsidies, they benefit little or not at all.

Most families save by paying off mortgages through homeownership and accumulating wealth in compounding retirement accounts. The automatic component of these assets—a monthly mortgage payment, regular deposits from earnings to savings—facilitate wealth building. Both methods are threatened by some disturbing current trends. The Great Recession led many low-income individuals to fear homeownership even when it became much cheaper on net than renting. Meanwhile mortgage credit has tightened—and might be further tightened with higher down payment rates—making credit most available in a bubble market and least in a bust market. For low-income families, especially families of color, this can exacerbate wealth inequality. Retirement savings, meanwhile, are threatened as a result of reduced employer contributions to pension plans and early employee withdrawals.

A common misconception is that poor or even low-income families cannot save. Research and evidence from savings programs show they can. When we examined families living below the poverty level, we found that over a decade more than 40 percent were able to increase their net worth and save enough to escape asset poverty—in other words, they had enough assets to live at the poverty level for three months without income (about $3,000 for an individual and $6,000 for a family of four).

The federal government spends hundreds of billions of dollars each year to support long-term asset development. But these asset-building subsidies primarily benefit high-income families, while low-income families receive next to nothing. Reforming policies like the mortgage interest tax deduction so it benefits all families, and helping families enroll in automatic savings vehicles, will help . . . promote savings opportunities for all Americans.

Periodical and Internet Sources Bibliography

The following articles have been selected to supplement the diverse views presented in this chapter.

Deborah Ashton	"Does Race or Gender Matter More to Your Paycheck?," *Harvard Business Review*, June 10, 2014.
American Association of University Women (AAUW)	"The Simple Truth About the Gender Pay Gap," Fall 2013.
Jamelle Bouie	"The Titanic Wealth Gap Between Blacks and Whites," *American Prospect*, February 27, 2013.
Bryce Covert	"The Ambition Myth: Debunking a Common Excuse for the Gender Wage Gap," *Atlantic*, December 3, 2012.
Diana Furchtgott-Roth	"The Gender Wage Gap Is a Myth," Market Watch, July 26, 2012.
Sophia Kerby	"How Pay Inequity Hurts Women of Color," Center for American Progress, April 9, 2013.
Carrie Lukas	"The 'Equal Pay Day' Myth," *Policy Focus*, vol. 2, no. 4, April 2012.
June O'Neill	"Race and Gender Wage Gaps: Discrimination Still to Blame?" *AEIdeas*, April 9, 2013.
Christina Hoff Sommers	"No, Women Don't Make Less Money than Men," The Daily Beast, February 1, 2014.
Thomas Sowell	"An Ignored 'Disparity,'" *Townhall*, January 17, 2012.

CHAPTER 3

What Causes Income Inequality?

Chapter Preface

Little debate surrounds the fact that income inequality in the United States has grown in recent decades, but debate about the causes of this growth in inequality is widespread. The Pew Research Center and *USA Today* conducted a political survey in January 2014. When they asked Americans whether they thought the gap between the rich and everyone else in the United States had increased, decreased, or stayed the same over the past decade, there was a strong consensus: 65 percent said it had increased, 25 percent said it had stayed the same, 8 percent said it had decreased, and 2 percent did not have an opinion. Among the almost two-thirds who said it had increased, however, little consensus emerged when asked *why* the increase had occurred.

The Pew Research Center and *USA Today* allowed respondents to give their own answers rather than supplying them with a list of possibilities. Three responses stood out, accounting for almost half the responses: fully one-fifth of those who believed income inequality had increased blamed the tax system or tax loopholes; one-tenth blamed Congress and government policies more generally; and 9 percent blamed the rise in income inequality on jobs or unemployment.

A host of other reasons came up. Some Americans blamed corporations and executives for the growth in inequality. Some saw banks, the housing market, or loans as the cause of growing inequality. Others saw the issue more in terms of morality, blaming greed, selfishness, fraud, and corruption. Some of those surveyed mentioned the power and opportunity of the rich as the cause of growing inequality, whereas others blamed the recession or the general economy. Some surveyed blamed the work ethic of the poor and government assistance programs; yet others credited the work ethic of the rich for the growing inequality. Many Americans saw the issue in political terms, blaming President Barack Obama, the Democrats, the Republicans, lobbyists, or regulation. Some respondents cited the education system as the cause, and others saw the cost of living as creating the inequality. Several other causes were cited, including capitalism, technology, weaker unions, health care, and immigration.

As the responses to this 2014 survey show, people hold a variety of beliefs about what led to the increase in income inequality over the past decade. Of course, it is possible that many causes have contributed to this inequality, and many of the answers given in the survey may be correct. Yet, not all causes cited are compatible with one another. As this survey and the authors of the viewpoints in this chapter illustrate, the debate about what causes income inequality is full of disagreement.

"A distinct aspect of rising inequality in
the United States is the wage gap between the very highest earners . . . and
other earners, including other high-
wage earners."

High Executive Compensation Has Increased Income Inequality

Lawrence Mishel and Natalie Sabadish

*In the following viewpoint, Lawrence Mishel and Natalie Sa-
badish argue that income inequality is largely driven by the
massive wage gap between the highest income earners and the
majority of US wage earners. Mishel and Sabadish claim that in
the past few decades, income inequality, executive compensation,
and the executive-to-worker ratio have all grown at alarming
rates. Mishel is president of the Economic Policy Institute, and
Sabadish is the Carnegie Mellon Fellow at the Center for American Progress.*

As you read, consider the following questions:

1. According to the authors, the significant income growth for top earners over the last few decades was driven by households headed by someone in one of what two jobs?

2. In 2011, according to Mishel and Sabadish, average CEO compensation with options realized was what amount per year?

3. According to the authors, in 1965, the CEO-to-worker compensation ratio was how much smaller than in 2000?

Growing income inequality has a number of sources, but a distinct aspect of rising inequality in the United States is the wage gap between the very highest earners—those in the upper 1.0 percent or even upper 0.1 percent—and other earners, including other high-wage earners. Driving this ever-widening gap is the unequal growth in earnings enjoyed by those at the top. The average annual earnings of the top 1 percent of wage earners grew 156 percent from 1979 to 2007; for the top 0.1 percent they grew 362 percent. In contrast, earners in the 90th to 95th percentiles had wage growth of 34 percent, less than a tenth as much as those in the top 0.1 percent tier. Workers in the bottom 90 percent had the weakest wage growth, at 17 percent from 1979 to 2007.

The Rise in Income Inequality

The large increase in wage inequality is one of the main drivers of the large upward distribution of household income to the top 1 percent, the others being the rising inequality of capital income and the growing share of income going to capital rather than wages and compensation. The result of these three trends was a more than doubling of the share of total income in the United States received by the top 1 percent between 1979 and 2007 and a large increase in the income gap between those at the top and the vast majority. In 2007, average annual incomes of the top 1 percent of households were 42 times greater than incomes of the bottom 90 percent (up from 14 times greater in 1979), and incomes of the top 0.1 percent were 220 times greater (up from 47 times greater in 1979).

Just as wage inequality is a key driver of income inequality, a key driver of wage inequality is the growth of chief executive officer [CEO] earnings and compensation and the expansion of and high compensation in the financial sector. This [viewpoint] uses data from EPI's [Economic Policy Institute's] upcoming "The State of Working America," 12th edition, to document and explain these trends. Our analysis first examines the role of executives and the financial sector in the growth of incomes of the top 1 percent and then presents new findings on the growth of CEO compensation back to 1965, including the growth of the CEO-to-worker compensation ratio.

The wages and compensation of executives, including CEOs, and of workers in finance reveal much about the rise in income inequality:

> The significant income growth at the very top of the income distribution over the last few decades was largely driven by households headed by someone who was either an executive or was employed in the financial sector. Executives, and workers in finance, accounted for 58 percent of the expansion of income for the top 1 percent and 67 percent of the increase in income for the top 0.1 percent from 1979 to 2005. These estimates understate the role of executive compensation and the financial sector in fueling income growth at the top because the increasing presence of working spouses who are executives or in finance is not included.

> From 1978 to 2011, CEO compensation increased more than 725 percent, a rise substantially greater than stock mar-

ket growth and the painfully slow 5.7 percent growth in worker compensation over the same period.

Using a measure of CEO compensation that includes the value of stock options granted to an executive, the CEO-to-worker compensation ratio was 18.3-to-1 in 1965, peaked at 411.3-to-1 in 2000, and sits at 209.4-to-1 in 2011.

Using an alternative measure of CEO compensation that includes the value of stock options exercised in a given year, CEOs earned 20.1 times more than typical workers in 1965, 383.4 times more in 2000, and 231.0 times more in 2011. . . .

CEO Compensation Trends

The 1980s, 1990s, and 2000s have been prosperous times for top U.S. executives, especially relative to other wage earners. The enormous pay increases received by chief executive officers of large firms has spillover effects (the pay of other executives and managers rises in tandem with CEO pay), but unfortunately no studies have established the scale of this impact. . . .

CEO compensation grew 78.7 percent between 1965 and 1978, three times the growth of the compensation of private-sector workers. It is interesting that the stock market (as measured by the Dow Jones and S&P indices) fell by about half at the same time. CEO compensation grew strongly over the 1980s but exploded in the 1990s and peaked in 2000 at more than $19 million, a growth of 1,279 or 1,390 percent, respectively, from 1978, with the options-realized and the options-granted measures. This growth in CEO compensation far exceeded even the substantial rise in the stock market, which grew 439 or 513 percent in value over the 1980s and 1990s. In stark contrast to both the stock market and CEO compensation growth was the 3.6 percent decline in the compensation of private-sector workers over the same period.

The fall in the stock market in the early 2000s led to a substantial paring back of CEO compensation, but by 2007

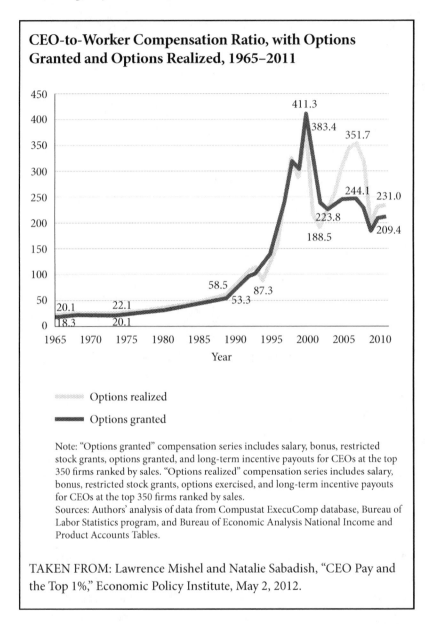

CEO-to-Worker Compensation Ratio, with Options Granted and Options Realized, 1965–2011

Note: "Options granted" compensation series includes salary, bonus, restricted stock grants, options granted, and long-term incentive payouts for CEOs at the top 350 firms ranked by sales. "Options realized" compensation series includes salary, bonus, restricted stock grants, options exercised, and long-term incentive payouts for CEOs at the top 350 firms ranked by sales.

Sources: Authors' analysis of data from Compustat ExecuComp database, Bureau of Labor Statistics program, and Bureau of Economic Analysis National Income and Product Accounts Tables.

TAKEN FROM: Lawrence Mishel and Natalie Sabadish, "CEO Pay and the Top 1%," Economic Policy Institute, May 2, 2012.

(when the stock market had mostly recovered) CEO compensation returned close to its 2000 levels, at least for the options-realized measure. The financial crisis in 2008 and the accompanying stock market tumble knocked CEO compensation down again. By 2011 the stock market had recouped a lot of ground lost in the 2008 financial crisis, and CEO compensation was $12.1 million measured with options realized and $11.1 million measured with options granted. CEO compensation grew roughly one percent in 2011 while a private-sector worker's compensation fell about one percent.

The CEO-to-Worker Compensation Ratio

CEO compensation in 2011 is very high by any metric, except when compared with its own peak in 2000, after the 1990s stock bubble. From 1978–2011, CEO compensation grew more than 725 percent, substantially more than the stock market and remarkably more than worker compensation, at a meager 5.7 percent. . . .

Depending on the CEO compensation measure, U.S. CEOs in major companies earned 20.1 or 18.3 times more than a typical worker in 1965; this ratio grew to 29.0-to-1 or 26.5-to-1 in 1978 and 58.5-to-1 or 53.3-to-1 by 1989 and then surged in the 1990s to hit 383.4-to-1 or 411.3-to-1 by the end of the recovery in 2000. The fall in the stock market after 2000 reduced CEO stock-related pay (e.g., options) and caused CEO compensation to tumble until 2002 and 2003. CEO compensation recovered to a level of 351.7 times worker pay by 2007, almost back to its 2000 level using the options-realized metric. The CEO-to-worker compensation ratio based on options granted, however, returned only to 244.1-to-1 in 2007, still far below its heights in 2000. The financial crisis in 2008 and accompanying stock market decline reduced CEO compensation after 2007–2008 . . . and the CEO-to-worker compensation ratio fell in tandem. By 2011 the stock market had recouped much of the value it lost following the financial crisis. Likewise, CEO compensation has grown from its 2009 low, and the CEO-to-worker compensation ratio has recovered to 231.0-to-1 or 209.4-to-1, depending on the measurement of options.

Though lower than in other years in the last decade, the CEO-to-worker compensation ratio in 2011 of more than 200-to-1 is far above the ratios prevailing in the 1960s, 1970s, 1980s, and mid-1990s. This illustrates that CEOs have fared far better than the typical worker, the stock market, or the U.S. economy over the last several decades. That begs the question: Is there any gauge against which to measure CEO pay that hasn't been surpassed?

> *"No amount of redistribution will reinvigorate the American dream or preserve the European system."*

Stop Obsessing over Exorbitant CEO Pay

Zachary Karabell

In the following viewpoint, Zachary Karabell argues that although the growth in income inequality is striking, the growth in wealth at the top of the income pyramid is not the cause of wage stagnation at the bottom. Karabell claims that researchers have been unable to prove a link between inequality and any harms to society. Furthermore, he contends that any attempt to lower executive compensation by redistribution will solve nothing. Karabell is the author of The Leading Indicators: A Short History of the Numbers That Rule Our World.

As you read, consider the following questions:

1. According to the author, a recent article in 2014 found the top executive earner to be making how much per year?

2. Karabell claims that the assumption of a causal link between excessive pay and stagnant lower incomes fuels the drive to make what tax change?

3. The author contends that inequality did not cause the middle class to lag and suffer; rather, he claims that inequality is a symptom of what?

L ast weekend [April 13, 2014] the *New York Times* published its annual list of executive compensation, with Oracle's Larry Ellison topping the charts at $78.4 million (and Disney's Bob Iger in a distant second, at $34.3 million). Pay packages have increased by an average of 9 percent since 2012, continuing a steady and spectacular rise even as average wages in the United States and throughout much of the developed world have stagnated.

The Assumption About Inequality

These figures are often presented as evidence in an ongoing debate that assumes a direct link between the accumulation of wealth at the top of the income pyramid and the stagnation of income for the vast middle and bottom. The *Times* article quotes the current leading critic of the inequities of global capitalism, *Capital in the Twenty-First Century* author Thomas Piketty: "The system is pretty much out of control in many ways."

That may be true. Business school professors who study the effect of excessive executive compensation [comp] are resoundingly convinced that too much comp hurts the overall performance of companies. Fifty years ago the ratio of average CEO [chief executive officer] comp to average salaries was 24-to-1; now it is 204-to-1. Many business scholars believe tying so much of CEO comp to stock and the performance of a company's shares incentivizes CEOs to make quarterly earnings look good whether or not it benefits the company's long-term health.

But does the widening gap between the pay of those at the top of the wealth heap and the rest *actually harm* those who are struggling or sinking? The underlying assumption tends to be an unequivocal yes. It's one of Piketty's claims—in sync with his overall view that capital benefits capital while chronically undermining wages and labor. Studies by University of California scholar Emmanuel Saez and Gabriel Zucman have been used as Exhibit A in the case for the pernicious influence of wealth inequality. These studies have been the subject of dozens of articles in the past month alone and are part of the corpus of evidence that accumulation of wealth is harming the middle class. Nobel Prize winner and former World Bank chief economist Joseph Stiglitz has made similar arguments.

A Lack of Evidence

But as *New York Times* economics writer Eduardo Porter noted recently, claiming that wealth inequality is unambiguously harmful is more about ideology than evidence. He cites the struggles of Harvard scholar Christopher Jencks, a leading chronicler of the middle class, to complete a planned book on income inequality. After years of research, Jencks was convinced that the only true statement about whether and how income inequality harms society is "It's hard to tell." Progressive economist Jared Bernstein has also found that we can't prove the assumption that inequality leads to slower growth, given available evidence. It *may* be true, Bernstein wrote, but we do not have enough concrete proof.

The work of Jencks and Bernstein complicates the neat narrative of robber barons and a new Gilded Age harming the middle class. Because those views lack black-and-white simplicity, however, they tend to receive less attention. Which is a shame, because they're probably closer to the truth.

The assumption of a causal link between excessive pay at the top and low growth and stagnant incomes fuels the drive to reframe the tax code toward greater redistribution. There is a strong moral case for that, especially insofar as massive gaps between the rich and the rest can be so insurmountable as to severely dent the idea of equality enshrined in the founding of the U.S. That said, even aggressive redistribution will not fundamentally solve what now ails us.

First, this is not an American phenomenon. Capital everywhere—from the corporate CEO in the U.S. to industrial titans in India to party leaders in China—is reaping the greatest rewards of global economic growth. Altering CEO pay structures would do little to alter that trajectory.

The Problem with Redistribution

The top 100 CEOs in the survey took home a total of $1.5 billion. That's rather nice for them, but redistributing, say, $1 billion of that would do almost nothing to help the 100 million people at the bottom of the economic pyramid in the U.S. Even if you included upper management and got to, let's say, $100 billion, the extra income distributed across American society would barely improve living standards. Boards could mandate that, say, Larry Ellison of Oracle should be less wealthy so that Oracle employees could be more wealthy, but Oracle employees are already on the winning side of the global economic equation. They are not the ones who need help.

Let's say then that you created an inequality tax, as Robert Shiller of Yale has proposed. That could certainly generate some extra billions, which could then be redistributed. But even there, the superrich would only become slightly less superrich, while those whose incomes are stagnating or those tens of millions underemployed and caught in a web of structural unemployment would see marginal improvement at best. In short, measures to reduce inequality might be modestly helpful, but they wouldn't solve much.

No matter what redistributive measures we took, we'd still be faced with an economic system in dramatic flux based on the erosion of traditional wage industries in the developed world over the past decades. It is not inequality that has caused the middle class to lag and suffer. Inequality rather is a symptom of a system that reached the limit of what it could provide wage earners performing jobs tied to 20th-century manufacturing.

Ballooning CEO pay is in turn a product of the globalization of capital, labor, and business (as Piketty highlights) without a commensurate evolution of some sort of global government and tax regime. Almost all of the companies that employ the top-paid CEOs are increasingly multinational and answer to no single government. That is a dramatic structural shift of the past two decades, driven by an emerging global middle class.

The focus on compensation has the virtue of a neat explanation for a real challenge. CEOs are paid egregiously; many, many people barely earn enough. But no amount of tweaking executive compensation will generate a vibrant, innovative economy. No amount of redistribution will reinvigorate the American dream or preserve the European system. Only if such tweaking goes hand in hand with a new growth engine—or a rethinking of the necessity of relentless growth—could it be constructive. Obsessing over executive compensation does nothing to contribute toward the hard work of making a generational transition away from the industrial economy that was and toward the information economy that will be.

> *"Income inequality in the US has risen to levels that threaten not only the economy's growth, but also the health of its democracy."*

Income Inequality Is Caused by Stagnating Middle-Class Incomes

Laura Tyson

In the following viewpoint, Laura Tyson argues that incomes in the United States have stagnated for several decades. She claims that slow wage growth among the middle class has slowed consumption and increased debt spending. Tyson raises concerns about the future of income inequality in the United States due to the lack of equal education opportunities and a political system dominated by money. Tyson, a former chair of the US president's Council of Economic Advisers, is a professor at the Haas School of Business at the University of California, Berkeley.

As you read, consider the following questions:

1. According to Tyson, average family income for the bottom 90 percent has been flat since what year?

2. How have middle- and lower-income households financed consumption over the past several decades, according to the author?

3. Tyson claims that between 1995 and 2012, the consumption share of the bottom 80 percent of earners dropped by how many percentage points?

During the last several decades, income inequality in the United States has increased significantly—and the trend shows no sign of reversing. The last time inequality was as high as it is now was just before the Great Depression. Such a high level of inequality is not only incompatible with widely held norms of social justice and equality of opportunity; it poses a serious threat to America's economy and democracy.

The US Middle Class

Underlying the country's soaring inequality is income stagnation for the majority of Americans. With an expanding share of the gains from economic growth flowing to a tiny fraction of high-income US households, average family income for the bottom 90% has been flat since 1980. According to a recent report by the Council of Economic Advisers, if the share of income going to the bottom 90% was the same in 2013 as it was in 1973, median annual household income (adjusted for family size) would be 18%, or about $9,000, higher than it is now.

The disposable (after tax and transfer) incomes of poor families in the US have trailed those of their counterparts in other developed countries for decades. Now the US middle class is also falling behind.

During the last three decades, middle-income households in most developed countries enjoyed larger increases in disposable income than comparable US households. This year [2014], the US lost the distinction of having the "most affluent" middle class to Canada, with several European countries not far behind. Once the generous public benefits in education, health care, and retirement are added to estimates of disposable family income in these countries, the relative position of the US middle class slips even further.

The Stagnation of Incomes

The main culprit behind the languishing fortunes of America's middle class is slow wage growth. After peaking in the early 1970s, real (inflation-adjusted) median earnings of full-time workers aged 25–64 stagnated, partly owing to a slowdown in productivity growth and partly because of a yawning gap between productivity and wage growth.

Since 1980, average real hourly compensation has increased at an annual rate of 1%, or half the rate of productivity growth. Wage gains have also become considerably more unequal, with the biggest increases claimed by the top 10% of earners.

Moreover, technological change and globalization have reduced the share of middle-skill jobs in overall employment, while the share of lower-skill jobs has increased. These trends, along with a falling labor-force participation rate during the last decade, explain the stagnation of middle-class incomes.

For most Americans, wages are the primary source of disposable income, which in turn drives personal consumption spending—by far the largest component of aggregate demand. Over the past several decades, as growth in disposable income slowed, middle- and lower-income households turned to debt to sustain consumption.

Personal savings rates collapsed, and credit and mortgage debt soared, as households attempted to keep pace with the consumption norms of the wealthy. For quite some time, growing income inequality did not slow consumption growth; indeed, "trickle-down consumption" pressures fostered more consumer spending, more debt, more bankruptcy, and more financial stress among middle- and lower-income households.

The Pattern of Recovery

The moment of reckoning arrived with the 2007–2008 financial crisis. Since then, aggregate consumption growth has been lackluster, as middle- and lower-income families have been forced to reduce their borrowing and pay down their debt, often through painful defaults on their homes—their primary (and often their only) asset.

As these families have tightened their belts, the pace of consumption spending and economic growth has become more dependent on earners at the top of the income distribution. Since the recession ended in 2009, real consumption spending by the top 5% has increased by 17%, compared to just 1% for the bottom 95%.

The recovery's pattern has reinforced longer-run trends. In 2012, the top 5% of earners accounted for 38% of personal-consumption expenditure, compared to 27% in 1995. During that period, the consumption share for the bottom 80% of earners dropped from 47% to 39%.

Looking to the future, growing income inequality and stagnant incomes for the majority of Americans mean weaker aggregate demand and slower growth. Even more important, income inequality constrains economic growth on the supply side through its adverse effects on educational opportunity and human-capital development.

The Negative Effects

Children born into low- and high-income families are born with similar abilities. But they have very different educational opportunities, with children in low-income families less likely to have access to early childhood education, more likely to attend under-resourced schools that deliver inferior K–12 education, and less likely to attend or complete college.

The resulting educational-attainment gap between children born into low- and high-income families emerges at an early age and grows over time. By some estimates, the gap today is twice as large as it was two decades ago. So the US is caught in a vicious circle: rising income inequality breeds more inequality in educational opportunity, which generates greater inequality in educational attainment. That, in turn, translates into a waste of human talent, a less educated workforce, slower economic growth, and even greater income inequality.

Although the economic costs of income inequality are substantial, the political costs may prove to be the most damaging and dangerous. The rich have both the incentives and the ability to promote policies that maintain or enhance their position.

Given the US Supreme Court's evisceration of campaign-finance restrictions, it has become easier than ever for concentrated economic power to exercise concentrated political power. Though campaign contributions do not guarantee victory, they give the economic elite greater access to legislators, regulators, and other public officials, enabling them to shape the political debate in favor of their interests.

As a result, the US political system is increasingly dominated by money. This is a clear sign that income inequality in the US has risen to levels that threaten not only the economy's growth, but also the health of its democracy.

> *"The best thing government can do to reduce income inequality is to get out of the way."*

Income Inequality Is Caused by Government Intervention

Ronald Bailey

In the following viewpoint, Ronald Bailey argues that when politicians intervene to reduce income inequality, they unintentionally make it worse. Bailey claims that, in the long run, income inequality will be reduced without government intervention. Government interventions that try to reduce inequality, he argues, decrease economic freedom and actually cause greater inequality. Bailey is the science correspondent for Reason *magazine and Reason.com, where he writes a weekly science and technology column.*

As you read, consider the following questions:

1. According to Bailey, the previous high-water mark for income inequality in the United States was in what year?

2. What eight states have the highest economic freedom, according to the author?

3. The author claims that research by the Fraser Institute shows that economic freedom has been in decline in most states since what year?

Income inequality has been attracting the attention of politicians, policy wonks, pundits, and the public. In 2013, President Barack Obama declared that "a dangerous and growing inequality" is the "defining challenge of our time." On *60 Minutes* last month [January 2015], Speaker of the House John Boehner argued that "the president's policies have made income inequality worse." Senator Mike Lee of Utah has said that "the United States is beset by a crisis in inequality" and that "bigger government is not the *solution* to unequal opportunity—it's the *cause*."

Economic Intervention and Inequality

In his 2013 speech, Obama also said, "We need to set aside the belief that government cannot do anything about reducing inequality." He's right, but not in the way he thinks. Several recent economic analyses show that the best thing government can do to reduce income inequality is to get out of the way.

For example, according to a study comparing outcomes in all U.S. states in the January 2014 issue of *Contemporary Economic Policy* by Illinois State University economist Oguzhan Dincer and his colleagues finds that reducing economic freedom actually tends to increase inequality. "On average, as the size and scope of government increases, so does income inequality," Dincer tells *Reason*.

The authors go on to establish "Granger causality." Simplistically stated, this means they show a causal feedback loop, in which economic intervention produces economic inequality, which in turn leads to more economic intervention. Politicians often react to rising inequality with policies that, on average, end up making inequality worse—say, by increasing the minimum wage. (That is not to say that some policies, such as raising the top marginal tax rate, could decrease inequality. But taken as a whole, the effect moves in the other direction.)

Income Inequality over Time

First consider the big picture. Progressives are fond of citing data that show that income inequality in the United States was falling throughout the 1950s and 1960s. The trend seemed to be following a hypothesis proposed by the economist Simon Kuznets. As economic growth takes off, Kuznets argued, income inequality initially increases as some workers move from low-productivity sectors into higher-productivity sectors. As the higher-productivity sectors absorb a growing proportion of workers, income inequality then begins to decrease, producing the famous inverse-U-shaped relationship between income inequality and economic growth.

The previous high-water mark for income inequality in the United States was in 1929, just before the Great Depression, when the Gini coefficient for household income inequality reached approximately 0.450. (If incomes were perfectly equal the Gini coefficient would be 0. If one household had all the income, it would be 1.) Income inequality decreased during the economic calamity of the Depression and continued to fall, just as Kuznets predicted, as the U.S. economy expanded in the post–World War II years. It hits a low point of 0.386 in 1968. At that point, according to data from the Federal Reserve Bank in St. Louis, the Gini coefficient began rising. By 1980 it reached 0.408, in 1990 it was 0.428, in 2000 it was 0.462, in 2010 it climbed to 0.470, and by 2013 it had ascended to 0.476.

A Canadian free-market think tank, the Fraser Institute, issues an annual report [called] the "Economic Freedom of North America," analyzing how each U.S. state and Canadian province stacks up with regard to measures such as taxation, government spending, and labor market freedom. Dincer's study analyzes trends in both economic freedom and income inequality among the states between 1981 and 2004, finding that "economic freedom reduces income inequality both in the short and the long run."

To get a rough idea of how this works, let's compare the eight states with the greatest economic freedom to the eight that scored the lowest. The eight states with the highest economic index scores, ranging from 7.8 to 7.1, were Texas, South Dakota, North Dakota, Virginia, New Hampshire, Louisiana, Nebraska, and Delaware. The eight states with the lowest scores, ranging from 5.2 to 5.8, were Maine, Vermont, Mississippi, New York, Rhode Island, West Virginia, New Jersey, and California. Averaging the U.S. Census Bureau's 2012 Gini coefficients for both groups, one finds that the Gini coefficient for the economically freer group is 0.452 whereas the one for the less free group is 0.469. In other words, income inequality is higher in the less economically free states.

A cautionary note: Dincer points out that a lot of information is lost when using just summary statistics like the freedom index. Still, an overall pattern can be detected. "I think the relationship between higher inequality and lower economic freedom is an indication of how badly state governments are being managed," Dincer suggests.

A Downward Spiral

A 2013 study in the *Journal of Regional Analysis and Policy* by economists at Ohio University and Florida State University bolsters Dincer's findings. That study, also using Fraser state economic freedom index data, identified a Kuznets curve relationship between increasing economic freedom and trends in income inequality. Their analysis "suggests that beginning from a low level of economic freedom, increases initially generate more inequality as the upper part of the income distribution benefits relatively more than the lower part; however, as enhancements of economic freedom continue, this reverses and the lower part of the distribution experiences larger relative income gains."

In their study, Dincer and his colleagues report that their results "support previous studies which find a positive relationship between economic freedom and per capita income." Last November, a National Bureau of Economic Research study by the Mississippi State University economist Travis Wiseman found, all things being equal, that a one-point increase on the Fraser "Economic Freedom of North America" index is associated with about an $8,156 increase in real average market incomes.

The most dismaying conclusion from Dincer's study is that its "results suggest that high income inequality may cause states to implement redistributive policies causing economic freedom to decline. As economic freedom declines, income inequality rises even more. In other words, it is quite possible for a state to get caught in a vicious circle of high income inequality and heavy redistribution." Sadly, the Fraser numbers show economic freedom in decline in most states since 2000.

In any case, the Gini coefficient rose in the eight least free states from an average 0.447 to 0.469 over that period. In contrast, the Gini coefficient increased at a slower rate, from an average of 0.439 to 0.452, for the eight freest states. In other words, the whole country appears to be on a downward spiral in which ever-lessening economic freedom produces ever-greater inequality.

> *"The most significant driver of that in-*
> *equality—the biggest impediment to*
> *upward economic mobility—isn't hard*
> *to identify."*

As Two-Parent Families Decline, Income Inequality Grows

Jeff Jacoby

In the following viewpoint, Jeff Jacoby argues that recent research shows that the poverty rate in single-parent homes is much higher than the poverty rate in married two-parent households. He claims that a strong association exists between growing up in an intact family and experiencing greater economic well-being both in childhood and adulthood. Jacoby contends that anyone concerned about income inequality in the United States needs to take this research seriously. Jacoby is an op-ed columnist at the Boston Globe.

As you read, consider the following questions:

1. Between 1980 and 2012, how much has the percentage of married two-parent households fallen, according to Jacoby?

2. According to Jacoby, for married adults raised in two-parent homes, household income is how much higher than their counterparts from single-parent homes?

3. According to the author, the median household income in Massachusetts in 2013 was how much less for single mothers than married couples?

Few political debates in this country are as freighted with emotional, cultural, and ideological baggage as those that touch on the choices people make in forming families. When public discourse turns to decisions about wedlock and child-rearing—think of Daniel Patrick Moynihan's 1965 report on "the breakdown of the Negro family," or the uproar over [single parenthood on TV show] *Murphy Brown* during the 1992 presidential race, or the modern push for same-sex marriage—civility is too often swept away amid a storm of hurt feelings and self-righteousness.

All the more reason, then, to welcome two recent studies—one national in scope, one focused on Massachusetts—on the effects of single parenthood and the decline in marriage. Both lay out the data with clarity, while avoiding moralizing or disapproval.

The Intact-Family Premium

One report, aptly titled "For Richer, For Poorer," is by sociologist W. Bradford Wilcox of the American Enterprise Institute and economist Robert I. Lerman of the Urban Institute. It documents the profound links that connect family structure and financial well-being and underscores what decades of empirical data have shown: Families headed by married couples tend to be much stronger economically than those headed by unwed single parents.

"Anyone concerned about family inequality, men's declining labor-force participation, and the vitality of the American dream should worry about the nation's retreat from marriage," the authors write. The steady fall in the percentage of married two-parent households—from 78 percent in 1980 to 66 percent in 2012—goes a long way toward explaining why so many ordinary families have trouble climbing beyond the lower rungs on the economic ladder. Correlation isn't proof of causation, of course. But there is no refuting the strong association between growing up with both parents in an intact family and achieving higher levels of education, work, and income as young adults.

Wilcox and Lerman put dollar amounts to the "intact-family premium" reaped by those who are raised by their own biological or adoptive parents. By age 28 to 30, for example, men from such backgrounds are earning on average $6,500 more per year in personal income than their peers from single-parent homes. And since growing up with both parents increases one's likelihood of marrying as an adult, men and women who were raised by married parents tend to enjoy much higher family incomes as well—in the case of that 28- to 30-year-old male, more than $16,000 higher, on average. (Among *all* married adults who were raised in a two-parent home, the annual average "family premium" is higher still: $42,000 more when compared to their counterparts from single-parent families.)

To be sure, not all families headed by married parents are stable or successful, and not all children raised by single parents struggle economically or professionally. Barack Obama, who was two years old when he was abandoned by his father, is dramatic evidence of that.

The Need to Understand Single Parenting

Single parenting as a cultural phenomenon represents not just a change in the way we view and judge ourselves as a society. Growing evidence suggests that it has implications far beyond that. The better we understand it, the closer we will be to understanding the challenging economic issues of poverty, income inequality and social mobility.

Aparna Mathur,
"The Biggest Reason for Income Inequality Is Single Parenthood,"
Forbes, *November 19, 2014.*

But as Obama himself says, the data aren't in question. "Children who grow up without a father are more likely to live in poverty. They're more likely to drop out of school. They're more likely to wind up in prison. They're more likely to abuse drugs and alcohol."

Poverty in Fatherless Homes

As the second study documents, these unhappy trends haven't bypassed Massachusetts.

In recent decades, the fraction of Bay State children in single-parent homes has risen to more than one in three. While the state's marriage rate has plummeted—there were 49,000 Bay State marriages in 1980 vs. fewer than 36,000 in 2011—the rate of out-of-wedlock births has soared. The Massachusetts Family Institute, in a report replete with just-the-facts-ma'am statistics, lays out the economic and social costs.

"The increase in fatherless families is a significant contributor to income inequality," it notes. In 2013, the median Massachusetts income for married-couple households with children was $114,376. For households headed by single mothers, it was just $26,999. Citing data from the National Survey of Children's Health, the report observes that only 6 percent of children in married-couple homes have no parent who works full-time. For kids being raised by never-married single mothers, the comparable figure is 46 percent.

There is no finger-wagging or blame in these reports, just the numbers—and compassion. The child poverty rate is so much steeper in single-parent homes than in two-parent homes, and it is heartbreaking that so many young people raised in fatherless families will have such trouble climbing out of poverty as they grow older.

Income inequality may or may not be "the defining challenge of our time," as Obama and others have proclaimed. But the most significant driver of that inequality—the biggest impediment to upward economic mobility—isn't hard to identify. The higher the fraction of children not being raised by their married parents, the more of our fellow citizens for whom the American dream is likely to remain beyond reach.

Periodical and Internet Sources Bibliography

The following articles have been selected to supplement the diverse views presented in this chapter.

Chuck Collins	"The Wealthy Kids Are All Right," *American Prospect*, vol. 24, no. 3, May–June 2013.
Peter Ferrara	"Obama's Rising Inequality," *American Spectator*, May 8, 2013.
Beverly Gage	"Radical Solutions to Economic Inequality," *Slate*, February 15, 2012.
Benjamin Landy	"A Tale of Two Recoveries: Wealth Inequality After the Great Recession," Century Foundation, August 28, 2013.
Marla McDaniel and Daniel Kuehn	"What Does a High School Diploma Get You? Employment, Race, and the Transition to Adulthood," *Review of Black Political Economy*, October 2012.
Sean McElwee	"The Right's New Charade: Blaming Single Mothers for Inequality," AlterNet, January 17, 2014.
Mark J. Perry and Michael Saltsman	"About That CEO/Employee Pay Gap," *Wall Street Journal*, October 12, 2014.
Nathan Pippenger	"The Thousand Fronts of Inequality," *Democracy*, November 12, 2014.
Thomas Sowell	"The Left's 'Income Inequality' Canard," *National Review*, April 24, 2014.
Thomas J. Sugrue	"A House Divided," *Washington Monthly*, January–February 2013.
Michael D. Yates	"The Great Inequality," *Monthly Review*, vol. 63, no. 10, March 2012.

OPPOSING
VIEWPOINTS®
SERIES

What Should Be Done About Income Inequality?

Chapter Preface

The Pew Research Center and *USA Today* conducted a political survey in January 2014 about economic inequality. This survey found the majority, 65 percent, in agreement with the view that the gap between rich and poor had increased in the previous ten years. However, when the Pew Research Center and *USA Today* asked this 65 percent about their viewpoint on what government can and should do about this gap, divisions were revealed.

When asked how much the government should do to reduce the gap between the rich and everyone else, partisan differences were striking. Whereas a large majority of Americans—69 percent—said that the government should do something to reduce the gap, a whopping 90 percent of Democrats agreed with this but only 45 percent of Republicans did. Among Republicans, 48 percent thought government should not do much or do nothing.

When asked about specific programs to reduce poverty, again there was division along party lines. When asked whether raising taxes on the wealthy and on corporations to expand programs for the poor would be effective in reducing poverty, just about half, 54 percent, favored doing so. Among Democrats, however, 75 percent thought raising taxes would be effective, whereas among Republicans only 29 percent thought so. When asked whether *lowering* taxes on the wealthy and corporations to encourage growth would be effective in reducing poverty, only 35 percent favored this, with 59 percent of Republicans believing this would be effective and only 17 percent of Democrats believing this.

Survey responses to other government policies showed similar political divisions. When asked if the government should raise the minimum wage to $10.10 an hour, a large majority, 73 percent, said it should. Yet only about half of Republicans (53 percent) and almost all Democrats (90 percent) expressed support for this government policy change. Almost as many Americans would like to see unemployment benefits extended—63 percent—with only 43 percent of Republicans and 83 percent of Democrats favoring this policy.

There are a variety of opinions about what should be done to address income inequality. As the authors of the viewpoints in this chapter demonstrate, not everyone thinks something should be done, and those who agree that things should change take a variety of different—and often competing—approaches.

> "In order to reform the system, we need a political movement for shared prosperity."

How to Shrink Inequality

Robert B. Reich

In the following viewpoint, Robert B. Reich argues that the level of inequality of income and wealth in the United States has reached the dangerous point where something must be done to reverse it. Reich contends that the current inequality is a threat to the economy, the ideal of equal opportunity, and democracy itself. He proposes ten initiatives to reverse the current trend. Reich is the Chancellor's Professor of Public Policy at the University of California at Berkeley and senior fellow at the Blum Center for Developing Economies.

As you read, consider the following questions:

1. According to the author, what percentage of economic activity in the United States is consumer spending?

2. Reich proposes raising the federal minimum wage to what amount per hour?

3. According to Reich, the richest 10 percent of Americans own what fraction of the value of the nation's capital stock?

Some inequality of income and wealth is inevitable, if not necessary. If an economy is to function well, people need incentives to work hard and innovate. The pertinent question is not whether income and wealth inequality is good or bad. It is at what point do these inequalities become so great as to pose a serious threat to our economy, our ideal of equal opportunity and our democracy.

The Widening Inequality

We are near or have already reached that tipping point. It is incumbent on us to dedicate ourselves to reversing this diabolical trend. It will not happen automatically, because the dysfunctions of our economy and politics are not self-correcting when it comes to inequality. In order to reform the system, we need a political movement for shared prosperity. Herewith, a short summary of what has happened, why it has happened, how it threatens the foundations of our society and what we must do to reverse it.

The data on widening inequality are remarkably and disturbingly clear. The Congressional Budget Office has found that between 1979 and 2007, the onset of the Great Recession, the gap in income—after federal taxes and transfer payments—more than tripled between the top 1 percent of the population and everyone else. The after-tax, after-transfer income of the top 1 percent increased by 275 percent, while it increased less than 40 percent for the middle three quintiles of the population and only 18 percent for the bottom quintile.

The gap has continued to widen in the recovery. According to the Census Bureau, median family and median household incomes have been falling, adjusted for inflation; while according to the data gathered by my colleague Emmanuel

Saez, the income of the wealthiest 1 percent has soared by 31 percent. In fact, Saez has calculated that 95 percent of all economic gains since the recovery began have gone to the top 1 percent.

Wealth has become even more concentrated than income. An April 2013 Pew Research Center report found that from 2009 to 2011, "the mean net worth of households in the upper 7 percent of wealth distribution rose by an estimated 28 percent, while the mean net worth of households in the lower 93 percent dropped by 4 percent."

The Threat to the Economy

This trend is now threatening the three foundation stones of our society: our economy, our ideal of equal opportunity and our democracy.

In the United States, consumer spending accounts for approximately 70 percent of economic activity. If consumers don't have adequate purchasing power, businesses have no incentive to expand or hire additional workers. Because the rich spend a smaller proportion of their incomes than the middle class and the poor, it stands to reason that as a larger and larger share of the nation's total income goes to the top, consumer demand is dampened. If the middle class is forced to borrow in order to maintain its standard of living, that dampening may come suddenly—when debt bubbles burst.

Consider that the two peak years of inequality over the past century—when the top 1 percent garnered more than 23 percent of total income—were 1928 and 2007. Each of these periods was preceded by substantial increases in borrowing, which ended notoriously in the Great Crash of 1929 and the near meltdown of 2008.

The anemic recovery we are now experiencing is directly related to the decline in median household incomes after 2009, coupled with the inability or unwillingness of consumers to take on additional debt and of banks to finance that debt—wisely, given the damage wrought by the bursting debt bubble. We cannot have a growing economy without a growing and buoyant middle class. We cannot have a growing middle class if almost all of the economic gains go to the top 1 percent.

The Ideal of Equal Opportunity

Widening inequality also challenges the nation's core ideal of equal opportunity, because it hampers upward mobility. High inequality correlates with low upward mobility. Studies are not conclusive because the speed of upward mobility is difficult to measure. But even under the unrealistic assumption that its velocity is no different today than it was thirty years ago—that someone born into a poor or lower-middle-class family today can move upward at the same rate as three decades ago—widening inequality still hampers upward mobility. That's simply because the ladder is far longer now. The distance between its bottom and top rungs, and between every rung along the way, is far greater. Anyone ascending it at the same speed as before will necessarily make less progress upward.

In addition, when the middle class is in decline and median household incomes are dropping, there are fewer possibilities for upward mobility. A stressed middle class is also less willing to share the ladder of opportunity with those below it. For this reason, the issue of widening inequality cannot be separated from the problems of poverty and diminishing opportunities for those near the bottom. They are one and the same.

The Undermining of Democracy

The connection between widening inequality and the undermining of democracy has long been understood. As former Supreme Court justice Louis Brandeis is famously alleged to have said in the early years of the last century, an era when robber barons dumped sacks of money on legislators' desks, "We may have a democracy, or we may have great wealth concentrated in the hands of a few, but we cannot have both."

As income and wealth flow upward, political power follows. Money flowing to political campaigns, lobbyists, think tanks, "expert" witnesses and media campaigns buys disproportionate influence. With all that money, no legislative bulwark can be high enough or strong enough to protect the democratic process.

The threat to our democracy also comes from the polarization that accompanies high levels of inequality. Partisanship—measured by some political scientists as the distance between median Republican and Democratic roll-call votes on key economic issues—almost directly tracks with the level of inequality. It reached high levels in the first decades of the twentieth century when inequality soared, and has reached similar levels in recent years.

When large numbers of Americans are working harder than ever but getting nowhere, and see most of the economic gains going to a small group at the top, they suspect the game is rigged. Some of these people can be persuaded that the culprit is big government; others, that the blame falls on the wealthy and big corporations. The result is fierce partisanship, fueled by anti-establishment populism on both the right and the left of the political spectrum.

The Flattening of Wages

Between the end of World War II and the early 1970s, the median wage grew in tandem with productivity. Both roughly doubled in those years, adjusted for inflation. But after the 1970s, productivity continued to rise at roughly the same pace as before, while wages began to flatten. In part, this was due to the twin forces of globalization and labor-replacing tech-

"A RISING TIDE LIFTS SOME BOATS..."

nologies that began to hit the American workforce like strong winds—accelerating into massive storms in the 1980s and '90s, and hurricanes since then.

Containers, satellite communication technologies and cargo ships and planes radically reduced the cost of producing goods anywhere around the globe, thereby eliminating many manufacturing jobs or putting downward pressure on other wages. Automation, followed by computers, software, robotics, computer-controlled machine tools and widespread digitization, further eroded jobs and wages. These forces simultaneously undermined organized labor. Unionized companies faced increasing competitive pressures to outsource, automate or move to nonunion states.

These forces didn't erode all incomes, however. In fact, they added to the value of complex work done by those who were well educated, well connected and fortunate enough to have chosen the right professions. Those lucky few who were perceived to be the most valuable saw their pay skyrocket.

A Lack of Response

But that's only part of the story. Instead of responding to these gale-force winds with policies designed to upgrade the skills of Americans, modernize our infrastructure, strengthen our safety net and adapt the workforce—and pay for much of this with higher taxes on the wealthy—we did the reverse. We began disinvesting in education, job training and infrastructure. We began shredding our safety net. We made it harder for many Americans to join unions. (The decline in unionization directly correlates with the decline of the portion of income going to the middle class.) And we reduced taxes on the wealthy.

We also deregulated. Financial deregulation in particular made finance the most lucrative industry in America, as it had been in the 1920s. Here again, the parallels between the 1920s and recent years are striking, reflecting the same pattern of inequality.

Other advanced economies have faced the same gale-force winds but have not suffered the same inequalities as we have because they have helped their workforces adapt to the new economic realities—leaving the United States the most unequal of all advanced nations by far.

Ten Proposed Initiatives

There is no single solution for reversing widening inequality. French economist Thomas Piketty has shown that rich nations are moving back toward the large wealth disparities that characterized the late nineteenth century, as the return on capital exceeds the rate of economic growth. His monumental book *Capital in the Twenty-First Century* paints a troubling picture of societies dominated by a comparative few, whose cumulative wealth and unearned income overshadow the majority who rely on jobs and earned income. But our future is not set in stone, and Piketty's description of past and current trends need not determine our path in the future. Here are ten initiatives that could reverse the trends described above:

1. *Make work pay.* The fastest-growing categories of work are retail, restaurant (including fast food), hospital (especially orderlies and staff), hotel, child care and elder care. But these jobs tend to pay very little. A first step toward making work pay is to raise the federal minimum wage to $15 an hour, pegging it to inflation; abolish the tipped minimum wage; and expand the earned income tax credit. No American who works full-time should be in poverty.

2. *Unionize low-wage workers.* The rise and fall of the American middle class correlates almost exactly with the rise and fall of private-sector unions, because unions gave the middle class the bargaining power it needed to secure a fair share of the gains from economic growth. We need to reinvigorate unions, beginning with low-wage service occupations that are sheltered from global competition and from labor-replacing technologies. Lower-wage Americans deserve more bargaining power.

3. *Invest in education.* This investment should extend from early childhood through world-class primary and secondary schools, affordable public higher education, good technical education and lifelong learning. Education should not be thought of as a private investment; it is a public good that helps both individuals and the economy. Yet for too many Americans, high-quality education is unaffordable and unattainable. Every American should have an equal opportunity to make the most of herself or himself. High-quality education should be freely available to all, starting at the age of 3 and extending through four years of university or technical education.

4. *Invest in infrastructure.* Many working Americans—especially those on the lower rungs of the income ladder—are hobbled by an obsolete infrastructure that generates long commutes to work, excessively high home and rental prices, inadequate Internet access, insufficient power and water sources and unnecessary environmental degradation. Every American should have access to an infrastructure suitable to the richest nation in the world.

5. *Pay for these investments with higher taxes on the wealthy.* Between the end of World War II and 1981 (when the wealthiest were getting paid a far lower share of total national income), the highest marginal federal income tax rate never fell below 70 percent, and the effective rate (including tax deductions and credits) hovered around 50 percent. But with Ronald Reagan's tax cut of 1981, followed by George W. Bush's tax cuts of 2001 and 2003, the taxes on top incomes were slashed, and tax loopholes favoring the wealthy were widened. The implicit promise—sometimes made explicit—was that the benefits from such cuts would trickle down to the broad middle class and even to the poor. As I've shown, however, nothing trickled down. At a time in American history when the after-tax incomes of the wealthy continue to soar, while median household incomes are falling, and when we must invest far more in education and infrastructure, it seems appropriate to raise the top marginal tax rate and close tax loopholes that disproportionately favor the wealthy.

6. *Make the payroll tax progressive.* Payroll taxes account for 40 percent of government revenues, yet they are not nearly as progressive as income taxes. One way to make the payroll tax more progressive would be to exempt the first $15,000 of wages and make up the difference by

removing the cap on the portion of income subject to Social Security payroll taxes.

7. *Raise the estate tax and eliminate the "stepped-up basis" for determining capital gains at death.* As Piketty warns, the United States, like other rich nations, could be moving toward an oligarchy of inherited wealth and away from a meritocracy based on labor income. The most direct way to reduce the dominance of inherited wealth is to raise the estate tax by triggering it at $1 million of wealth per person rather than its current $5.34 million (and thereafter peg those levels to inflation). We should also eliminate the "stepped-up basis" rule that lets heirs avoid capital gains taxes on the appreciation of assets that occurred before the death of their benefactors.

8. *Constrain Wall Street.* The financial sector has added to the burdens of the middle class and the poor through excesses that were the proximate cause of an economic crisis in 2008, similar to the crisis of 1929. Even though capital requirements have been tightened and oversight strengthened, the biggest banks are still too big to fail, jail or curtail—and therefore capable of generating another crisis. The Glass-Steagall Act, which separated commercial- and investment-banking functions, should be resurrected in full, and the size of the nation's biggest banks should be capped.

9. *Give all Americans a share in future economic gains.* The richest 10 percent of Americans own roughly 80 percent of the value of the nation's capital stock; the richest 1 percent own about 35 percent. As the returns to capital continue to outpace the returns to labor, this allocation of ownership further aggravates inequality. Ownership should be broadened through a plan that would give every newborn American an "opportunity share" worth, say, $5,000 in a diversified index of stocks and bonds—

which, compounded over time, would be worth considerably more. The share could be cashed in gradually starting at the age of 18.

10. *Get big money out of politics.* Last, but certainly not least, we must limit the political influence of the great accumulations of wealth that are threatening our democracy and drowning out the voices of average Americans. The Supreme Court's 2010 *Citizens United [v. Federal Election Commission]* decision must be reversed—either by the court itself, or by constitutional amendment. In the meantime, we must move toward the public financing of elections—for example, with the federal government giving presidential candidates, as well as House and Senate candidates in general elections, $2 for every $1 raised from small donors.

A Movement for Shared Prosperity

It's doubtful that these and other measures designed to reverse widening inequality will be enacted anytime soon. Having served in Washington, I know how difficult it is to get anything done unless the broad public understands what's at stake and actively pushes for reform.

That's why we need a movement for shared prosperity—a movement on a scale similar to the Progressive movement at the turn of the last century, which fueled the first progressive income tax and antitrust laws; the suffrage movement, which won women the vote; the labor movement, which helped animate the New Deal and fueled the great prosperity of the first three decades after World War II; the civil rights movement, which achieved the landmark Civil Rights and Voting Rights Acts; and the environmental movement, which spawned the National Environmental Policy Act and other critical legislation.

Time and again, when the situation demands it, America has saved capitalism from its own excesses. We put ideology

aside and do what's necessary. No other nation is as fundamentally pragmatic. We will reverse the trend toward widening inequality eventually. We have no choice. But we must organize and mobilize in order that it be done.

> "We ought not to preoccupy ourselves
> with the rise in income inequality over
> the past several decades because it has
> affected neither economic mobility nor
> economic growth."

The Misguided Focus on
Income Inequality

David Azerrad and Rea S. Hederman Jr.

*In the following viewpoint, David Azerrad and Rea S. Heder-
man Jr. argue that the outrage about income inequality is misguided, as income inequality in itself is not indicative of a problem. In fact, they claim, income is not a good measure of well-
being and an increase in income inequality does not threaten the
American dream. Azerrad is director of the Heritage Foundation's
B. Kenneth Simon Center for Principles and Politics. Hederman
is executive vice president and chief operating officer of the
Buckeye Institute for Public Policy Solutions.*

As you read, consider the following questions:

1. The authors contend that there would be reason to be concerned about income inequality only if the rich had grown richer how?

2. To what has President Obama linked the rise in inequality, according to the viewpoint?

3. According to the authors, 79 percent of those who are poor failed to do what three things?

The politics of income inequality is all the rage with the Left these days. The claim that we now live in a "New Gilded Age" has become a staple of liberal discourse. President Barack Obama has called growing inequality "the defining challenge of our time." So spectacular are the increases in inequality that they have "no counterpart anywhere else in the advanced world," laments the *New York Times*'s Paul Krugman. "Economically speaking," Timothy Noah writes in *The Great Divergence*, "the richest nation on earth is starting to resemble a banana republic."

The Outrage About Income Inequality

The astute observer will notice that many of those who rail against inequality either do not bother to explain why inequality is bad or do so as a mere afterthought. The main focus is almost always the fact that disparities in income are more pronounced today than they were in the 1970s. Krugman, for example, wrote an entire book about the "New Gilded Age" in which he never explains why Americans ought to be concerned about inequality. What stokes his outrage is the mere fact that some have become richer than others.

There is one glaring problem with this approach: In and of itself, income inequality is meaningless. It is a brute fact that may or may not be indicative of a deeper problem. A claim about inequality without a sustained discussion of its effects and causes tells us very little. If anything, we as Americans ought to be less suspicious than others of income inequalities. In *The Federalist,* "the greatest work of American political thought," James Madison defined the "*first* object of Government" as "the protection of different and *unequal* faculties of acquiring property," from which result "different degrees and kinds of property."

To state the obvious, enforced income parity is neither desirable nor just. Because people have different native talents, upbringings, and interests, an economy in which they are free to buy, sell, trade, manufacture, produce, and invest in what they please will inevitably lead to great inequalities of wealth and income.

That is not to say, of course, that inequalities are always the result of normal market forces. It may well be that unjust economic regulations arbitrarily deny certain segments of the population the full liberty to exercise their rights and in turn lead to disparities in income. It may also be that some have devised an ingenuous illegal way to make a lot of money. But the problem in such cases, and in any other similar ones, lies with the unjust regulation or the illegal business practice, not with the resulting inequality. Inequality may be a symptom of deeper structural injustice. Or it may not.

In our case in America, it seems that globalization and technological advances have been the main drivers of rising incomes at the very top. With the fall of communism, the integration of China and India into world markets, trade has become much freer in recent decades. And thanks to technology it has also become much faster. There are now more consumers and more ways to deliver products and services to them (e.g., the Internet). The expansion of markets, combined with the lowering of marginal tax rates—from 70% in 1980 to 39.6% today—creates a superstar effect at the top.

Inequality is rising not because the wealthy have become better at fleecing the poor. Inequality is rising because those

---

The American Dream vs. the Liberal Dream

Two Conflicting Dreams	The American Dream	The Liberal Dream
Symbol	Ladder of opportunity	Escalator of results
Aim	Ensure all have the opportunity to rise	Ensure all actually rise
Primary focus	Individual effort	Government assistance
Role of government	Supporting role	Primary role
Source of opportunity	Free markets	Government spending
Type of opportunity	Remove artificial barriers to ensure equal opportunity	Social engineering to achieve sameness of opportunity
Primary threat	Government dependence	Income inequality

TAKEN FROM: David Azerrad and Rea S. Hederman Jr., "Defending the Dream: Why Income Inequality Doesn't Threaten Opportunity," Special Report, no. 119, Heritage Foundation, September 13, 2012.

---

who aspire to become formidably wealthy today can expect to earn a whole lot more than people who aspired to become formidably wealthy a generation ago would have.

A simple example can illustrate this. Whereas Nolan Ryan only made a little over $1 million a year in 1979 when he became the first-ever baseball millionaire, Clayton Kershaw, the highest-paid player today, makes $30 million a year.

The Rich and the Poor

Rather than obsess over the incomes of the wealthy, we should focus our attention instead on the poor and the middle class. The income inequality numbers look at how the different income segments in society relate to each other, but they tell us nothing about what really matters: the number of Americans who are living in poverty, their quality of life, and the opportunities available to all Americans. What matters is not how much more those at the top earn in relation to those at the bottom—they are, after all, not in competition with one another—but rather the real needs of those at the bottom and their opportunities for advancement.

The needs of the poor have nothing to do with the earnings of the rich. There are broadly agreed upon standards of what a decent life looks like, and while these standards will change over time and vary by country—indoor plumbing is no longer considered a luxury item in the U.S.; it still is in Somalia—they are not defined in relation to how much the richest 1 percent of the country earn. People like Bill Gates and Warren Buffett can make as much money as they want, but, so long as they earned their money honestly, what do their earnings have to do with the quality of life for the rest of us?

If it were the case that the rich had grown richer at the expense of the poor, thereby making them poorer, then we would have reason to be concerned. That, however, is not the way our economy generally works. A free-market economy creates wealth. For one person to make a dollar does not mean that another needs to lose one. There is not just one dwindling pie to be divided up among the population, but rather a proven recipe to grow the pie to serve everyone. All the talk about the rich "grabbing" too large a share of the national income therefore rests on a flawed understanding of this basic truth of free-market economics.

The Rise in Income

In recent decades, income has risen for *all* segments of the population. A recent study by the nonpartisan Congressional Budget Office analyzed the changes in after-tax income for different segments of the population from 1979 to 2007. Aftertax income rose by:

- 18 percent for the bottom 20 percent of households,

- just under 40 percent for the next 60 percent,

- 65 percent for the next 19 percent, and

- 275 percent for the top 1 percent.

Only if you were to assume mistakenly that free-market economics promises to raise standards of living equally for all rather than to raise them in general would you be worried about the unequal growth rates. And only if you were driven primarily by resentment of the rich rather than by a genuine concern for the well-being of all Americans would you zero in on the gains of the 1 percent.

The excessive focus on the 1 percent of income earners is particularly reflective of a certain mind-set. Envy, not compassion, seems to be the animating passion of many of those who worry about inequality. They begin with the rich—the Sort of Rich, the Basically Rich, the Undeniably Rich, the Really Rich, and the Stinking Rich in Timothy Noah's classification—not with the poor or the middle class. They focus on the top 1 percent, not the bottom 1 percent, and when the wealth of the 1 percent no longer sufficiently stokes their outrage, they hone in on ever smaller subsets of the rich. Thomas Piketty and Emmanuel Saez, the great economists of income inequality, tabulate incomes of the top 1 percent, the top 0.5 percent, the top 0.1 percent, and even the top 0.01 percent.

Income Inequality and the American Dream

To be fair to the Left, the more thoughtful liberals who worry about income inequality do actually put forward an argument as to why it matters. It is not all seething resentment against the rich and alarmist claims about our slow descent into plutocracy. Some actually try to make the case for the damaging consequences of inequality. President Barack Obama, for example, has linked the rise in inequality to a decline in opportunity:

> "This kind of gaping inequality gives [the] lie to the promise that's at the very heart of America: that this is a place where you can make it if you try. . . . [O]ver the last few decades, the rungs on the ladder of opportunity have grown farther and farther apart, and the middle class has shrunk."

Such claims were dubious then as no one bothered to explain how the growth in the earnings of the wealthy somehow diminished the prospects of the poor to lift themselves out of poverty. Why would a child from a poor family be less likely to graduate high school, avoid drugs, go to college, not have children out of wedlock and find a job if the average income of the top 0.1% of earners quintupled over the past three decades?

These claims are now even less plausible in light of massive recent studies led by Harvard's Raj Chetty indicating that upward mobility in America has not declined in spite of the rise in inequality. As he and his colleagues concluded, after poring over millions of IRS [Internal Revenue Service] tax records: "children entering the labor market today have the same chances of moving up in the income distribution (relative to their parents) as children born in the 1970s."

Others have tried to hang their hat on the claim that rising inequality threatens economic growth. The evidence is rather inconclusive. According to the Washington Center for Equitable Growth, a progressive think tank devoted to the study of inequality and growth: "the overall findings in this academic arena are mixed. Inequality has been found to reduce growth, boost growth or have no effect at all. The varying methods used in these papers end up producing a variety of results."

In sum, the evidence demonstrates that:

1. Income inequality has indeed risen in recent decades, but

   a. The standard measure of income based on Census Bureau data is flawed. A more precise measure reveals that income inequalities are not as pronounced as the standard measures suggest.

   b. Income is not a good measure of well-being, but consumption is—and the material quality of life has increased for all, regardless of income. We live longer, have bigger homes, better technology and more amenities.

2. The rise in income inequality has not been orchestrated but is the result of changes in the economy.

3. The rise in income inequality has not led to a decline in economic mobility nor to an economic slowdown.

The Real Recipe for Success

The decline in income inequality brought about by the recent recession illustrates the danger of relying on income equality as an index of the country's health. Because wealthy families were hit harder by the recession, their income declined more rapidly than the income of poorer families. Income inequality decreased, but so did overall prosperity. If we follow the lead of the income equalizers, we ought to be cheering.

This is absurd. In reality, we ought not to preoccupy ourselves with the rise in income inequality over the past several decades because it has affected neither economic mobility nor economic growth. Standards of living have increased for everyone—as have incomes, for that matter—and mobility, whichever way you measure it, remains robust. Countless Americans are still making it every year through hard work, perseverance, and dedication.

The recipe for success has not changed over the years. To ensure the best opportunity for mobility, you should at least graduate high school, wait to be married before having children, obey the law, and avoid self-destructive behavior such as drug and alcohol abuse. Involvement in religious and other community organizations that form character also increases the likelihood that someone will move up the ladder.

Getting more education is one of the best ways to ensure that you can surpass your parents and your peers. A recent study found that having a college education makes children significantly more likely to surpass their parents in income and wealth and less likely to experience downward mobility.

For those who are concerned with avoiding poverty, the rules are even simpler. As former [Bill] Clinton adviser William Galston summed it up, "you need only do three things in this country to avoid poverty—finish high school, marry before having a child, and marry after the age of 20." Only 8 percent of these families are poor, whereas 79 percent of those who fail to do this are poor.

> "Political-economic inequality should be
> ended by repealing all privileges right
> now."

Only Political Inequality, Not Market Inequality, Should Be Eliminated

Sheldon Richman

In the following viewpoint, Sheldon Richman argues that there are two kinds of economic inequality and only one needs to be eliminated. Market inequality created by different personal talents does not need to be eliminated, says Richman, whereas inequality fostered through the political system that creates artificial benefits for some should be eliminated. Richman is the author of Separating School & State: How to Liberate America's Families; Your Money or Your Life: Why We Must Abolish the Income Tax; *and* Tethered Citizens: Time to Repeal the Welfare State.

As you read, consider the following questions:

1. According to the author, in a market-oriented economy some people will make more money for what reason?

2. Richman claims that favors in a market-oriented system that stem from privilege typically go to whom?

3. What are some ways that Richman suggests political-economic inequality could be eliminated? Name at least two.

Income inequality is back in the news, propelled by an Oxfam International report and President Barack Obama's State of the Union address. The question is whether government needs to do something about this—or whether government needs to *undo* many things.

Two Kinds of Economic Inequality

Measuring income inequality is no simple thing, which is one source of disagreement between those who think inequality is a problem and those who think it isn't. But it is possible to cut through the underbrush and make some points clear.

We can identify two kinds of economic inequality, and let's keep this in mind as we contemplate what, if anything, government ought to do.

The first kind we might call market inequality. Individuals differ in many ways, including energy, ambition, and ingenuity. As a result, in a market-oriented economy some people will be better than others at satisfying consumers and will hence tend to make more money. The only way to prevent that is to interfere forcibly with the results of peaceful, positive-sum transactions in the marketplace. Since interference discourages the production of wealth, the equality fostered through violence will be an equality of impoverishment.

Is it better that people be equally poor or unequally affluent? This is the important question that political philosopher John Tomasi, author of *Free Market Fairness*, puts to his classes at Brown University. Would they prefer a society in which everyone has the same *low* income, or one in which incomes vary, perhaps widely, but the lowest incomes are higher than the equal income of the first society?

Which would you choose? Let's remember that it is entirely possible for the poorest in a society to become richer even as the gap between the richest and poorest grows. Imagine an accordion-like elevator that is rising as a whole while being stretched out, putting the floor further from the ceiling. Would such a society be objectionable? Why is the relative position of the poorest more important than their absolute position? Is concern about relative positions nothing more than envy?

Political-Economic Inequality

We could argue about that all day, but a much more urgent subject is political-economic inequality. This is the inequality fostered through the political system. Since government's distinctive feature is its claimed authority to use force aggressively (as opposed to defensively), this second sort of inequality is produced by violence, which on its face should make it abhorrent.

Political-economic systems throughout the world, including ones typically thought to be market oriented (or "capitalist"), such as in the United States, are in fact built on deeply rooted and long-established systems of privilege. Favors, which the rest of us must pay for one way or another, typically go to the well connected, and prominent business executives have always been well represented in that group.

In the United States, this has been true since the days of John Jacob Astor, the fur trader who had the ears of such influential politicians as James Madison, James Monroe, and John Quincy Adams. Government was little more than the executive committee of leading manufacturers, planters, and merchants (to risk opprobrium by paraphrasing [Karl] Marx). As Adam Smith put it in *The Wealth of Nations* in 1776,

"Whenever the legislature attempts to regulate the differences between masters and their workmen, its counsellors are always the masters."

While business interests today are not the only ones that get consideration in the halls of power, it's a mistake to think they do not retain major influence over government in economic and financial matters. "Regulatory capture" is a well-known phenomenon, and ostensible efforts to limit it always fail.

The Elimination of Political-Economic Inequality

Unlike market inequality, political-economic inequality is unjust and should be eliminated.

How? By abolishing all direct and indirect subsidies; artificial scarcities, such as those created by so-called intellectual property; regulations, which inevitably burden smaller and yet-to-be-launched firms more than lawyered-up big businesses; eminent domain; and permit requirements, zoning, and occupational licensing, which all exclude competition. These interventions and more protect incumbent firms from conditions that would lower prices to consumers, create self-employment and worker-ownership opportunities, and improve bargaining conditions for wage labor.

Instead of symbolically tweaking the tax code to appear to be addressing inequality—the politicians' charade—political-economic inequality should be ended by repealing all privileges right now.

> "There's a path to closing the gap, fo-
> cused more on increasing opportunity
> than equalizing outcomes."

Quality Education Would Improve Income Inequality

Josh Kraushaar

In the following viewpoint, Josh Kraushaar argues that the best way to increase economic mobility, thereby decreasing inequality, is by increasing access to good education. Kraushaar claims that too often initiatives to improve public education are opposed by politicians. He claims that the rhetoric about income inequality is often political and avoids the key solutions of improving public education and access to college. Kraushaar is the political editor for National Journal *and writes the weekly* Against the Grain *column.*

As you read, consider the following questions:

1. Kraushaar claims that progressives typically only discuss the demand part of education, ignoring what three efforts on the supply side?

2. According to the author, what three steps did New Orleans take to reform its public schools, leading to increased test scores and graduation rates?

3. What proposal from the Obama administration does the author claim would offer little economic benefit?

For progressives, the buzzy phrase of the moment is income inequality. President [Barack] Obama plans to make it the focus of his upcoming State of the Union address after sermonizing about the issue in December [2013]. New York City mayor Bill de Blasio made it the centerpiece of his campaign and the theme of his inauguration ceremony. Freshman Massachusetts [senator] Elizabeth Warren gained national celebrity because of her outspoken criticism of moneyed interests.

The Need for Quality Education

But as these politicians are invoking the issue for political gain, they're avoiding one prescription that has proven to be a time-tested path to economic mobility—increasing access to *quality* education. When progressives discuss education, it frequently leads to the demand part of the equation. De Blasio proposed offering universal pre-K and after-school to city residents, while Obama has made it easier for students to obtain grants and loans to tackle the skyrocketing cost of a college education.

Left unmentioned are the efforts on the supply side—expanding school choice, improving teacher quality, and strengthening curriculum. In most poor, city neighborhoods, students are locked into failing schools, with few options for parents to turn to. Unions are invested in protecting an educational monopoly, fearing that increased competition could drag down salaries and threaten employment for less-than-qualified teachers. At the college level, one major culprit for rising tuition is that government is aggressively subsidizing tuition costs—spurring inflation—without demanding accountability from the universities benefiting. As the bar to attending a four-year college has been lowered, fewer students are graduating and more are exiting with calamitous debt, degree or no degree.

The victims of this bubble are the students. Politicians benefit from feel-good rhetoric, administrators see a steady flow of money filling their coffers, and teachers can rest assured their jobs are protected regardless of their abilities in the classroom. All the pre-K and low-interest tuition loans in the world won't matter if the education being provided is substandard.

The Opposition to Education Initiatives

Yet, those railing against economic inequality are doing very little to offer an educational pathway for children to rise out of poverty. De Blasio has declared war against charter schools in New York City, proposing to stunt their growth in the city by threatening to stop offering them free rent. More brazenly, the Obama Justice Department filed a lawsuit against a Louisiana program designed to allow poor students to pick alternatives to their failing public schools. It's on par with the administration's hostility to school choice: One of the first moves the Obama administration made was trying to shut down the popular D.C. Opportunity Scholarship Program, providing vouchers to city students to attend private schools.

Last April, my colleague Adam Kushner documented the remarkable turnaround New Orleans public schools are experiencing, thanks to a wave of educational reforms introduced in the wake of Hurricane Katrina. The city laid off most of its public school teaching workforce, liberally issued charter school licenses, and demanded accountability from its students. In a system that's 95 percent black and with 92 percent of students getting free or reduced lunches, the passing rate on state tests nearly doubled and the graduation rate is now higher than the national average.

Such reforms aren't a panacea for the numerous challenges facing impoverished Americans. As Kushner wrote, the New Orleans school system has gone from a "state of crisis to a state of mediocrity, which counts as a miracle here." For every successful KIPP college-prep charter school in the city, there's another charter school that's flailing down the road. But the successes clearly demonstrate a pathway for success—one that holds a much better track record than simply spending more money without setting necessary benchmarks.

Despite de Blasio's hostility to education reform, it has become something of a necessity for Democratic mayors across the country. Many cities, like Washington, are experiencing an economic and cultural renaissance thanks to an influx of young professionals eager to tap into their vibrant environment. But without an adequate public school system, many families will move out when they have school-age kids. Many of the party's leading mayors, from Chicago's Rahm Emanuel to Michael Nutter in Philadelphia, have been charter school boosters. Former Newark mayor Cory Booker, now New Jersey's junior senator, has even backed vouchers for private and parochial education.

A Political Issue

It's telling that the first big pitch from the Obama administration and down-ballot Democratic candidates in 2014 is a push for raising the minimum wage—an issue that's famous for its political value but offers little in the way of economic benefit. (Two experts on the subject argue it helps low-skilled workers who keep their jobs at the expense of others looking for work.) By contrast, education reform is one of the rare issues that could unite a cross-section of Republicans and Democrats. It would allow the president to build a bipartisan alliance while tackling his signature pitch on income inequality.

In reality, the White House's rhetoric about income inequality is as much about politics as policy. Obama unveiled his first speech on the subject during the 2012 campaigns— long after the Occupy Wall Street movement [a protest movement against social and economic inequality] sprang up on the left—as a way to hit Mitt Romney for his plutocratic background. "The themes he laid out were tailor-made for a campaign," authors Mark Halperin and John Heilemann wrote in their campaign opus *Double Down*. Indeed, Obama rarely promotes his administration's Race to the Top initiative incentivizing states to raise educational standards—he devoted just one sentence to it in his income inequality speech—because the program irks the party's teachers' union allies.

The tougher challenge is to advance policies that address a major reason behind the growing educational gap—the fact that poorer children aren't afforded the same educational opportunities as wealthier ones. There's a path to closing the gap, focused more on increasing opportunity than equalizing outcomes. But it means the president and his progressive allies will have to make decisions to move beyond speeches and the minimum wage.

> "Rising inequality isn't about who has the knowledge; it's about who has the power."

Knowledge Isn't Power

Paul Krugman

In the following viewpoint, Paul Krugman argues that it is false that economic growth is being stunted and income inequality is fueled by a lack of adequate education. Krugman contends that there is no evidence of the so-called skills gap behind this argument. He says that rising inequality is about the rise of power within a tiny group of people and that such inequality of power must be addressed. Krugman is professor of economics and international affairs at the Woodrow Wilson School of Public and International Affairs at Princeton University as well as op-ed columnist for the New York Times.

As you read, consider the following questions:

1. What is the so-called skills gap that Krugman says is part of the education-centric story of inequality?

2. According to Krugman, in what job sector were there the biggest recent wage gains?

3. What two suggestions does Krugman offer for how inequality of power could be redressed?

Regular readers know that I sometimes mock "very serious people"—politicians and pundits who solemnly repeat conventional wisdom that sounds tough-minded and realistic. The trouble is that sounding serious and being serious are by no means the same thing, and some of those seemingly tough-minded positions are actually ways to dodge the truly hard issues.

The Education-Centric Story

The prime example of recent years was, of course, Bowles-Simpsonism [referring to the National Commission on Fiscal Responsibility and Reform, headed by senators Alan Simpson and Erskine Bowles]—the diversion of elite discourse away from the ongoing tragedy of high unemployment and into the supposedly crucial issue of how, exactly, we will pay for social insurance programs a couple of decades from now. That particular obsession, I'm happy to say, seems to be on the wane. But my sense is that there's a new form of issue-dodging packaged as seriousness on the rise. This time, the evasion involves trying to divert our national discourse about inequality into a discussion of alleged problems with education.

And the reason this is an evasion is that whatever serious people may want to believe, soaring inequality isn't about education; it's about power.

Just to be clear: I'm in favor of better education. Education is a friend of mine. And it should be available and affordable for all. But what I keep seeing is people insisting that educational failings are at the root of still-weak job creation, stagnating wages and rising inequality. This sounds serious and thoughtful. But it's actually a view very much at odds with the evidence, not to mention a way to hide from the real, unavoidably partisan debate.

The education-centric story of our problems runs like this: We live in a period of unprecedented technological change, and too many American workers lack the skills to cope with that change. This "skills gap" is holding back growth, because businesses can't find the workers they need. It also feeds inequality, as wages soar for workers with the right skills but stagnate or decline for the less educated. So what we need is more and better education.

An Implausible Story

My guess is that this sounds familiar—it's what you hear from the talking heads on Sunday morning TV, in opinion articles from business leaders like Jamie Dimon of JPMorgan Chase, in "framing papers" from the Brookings Institution's centrist Hamilton Project. It's repeated so widely that many people probably assume it's unquestionably true. But it isn't.

For one thing, is the pace of technological change really that fast? "We wanted flying cars, instead we got 140 characters," the venture capitalist Peter Thiel has snarked. Productivity growth, which surged briefly after 1995, seems to have slowed sharply.

Furthermore, there's no evidence that a skills gap is holding back employment. After all, if businesses were desperate for workers with certain skills, they would presumably be offering premium wages to attract such workers. So where are these fortunate professions? . . . Interestingly, some of the biggest recent wage gains are for skilled manual labor—sewing machine operators, boilermakers—as some manufacturing production moves back to America. But the notion that highly skilled workers are generally in demand is just false.

Finally, while the education/inequality story may once have seemed plausible, it hasn't tracked reality for a long time.

A Wage Deficit, Not a Skills Deficit

The huge increase in wage and income inequality experienced over the last 30 years is not a reflection of a shortfall in the skills and education of the workforce. Rather, workers face a wage deficit, not a skills deficit. It is hard to find some ever-increasing need for college graduates that is going unmet: College graduates have not seen their real wage rise in 10 years, and the pay gap with high school graduates has not increased in that time period. Moreover, even before the recession, college students and graduates were working as free interns, a phenomenon we would not observe if college graduates were in such demand.

Lawrence Mishel, "Education Is Not the Cure for High Unemployment or for Income Inequality," Economic Policy Institute, Briefing Paper, no. 286, January 12, 2011.

"The wages of the highest-skilled and highest-paid individuals have continued to increase steadily," the Hamilton Project says. Actually, the inflation-adjusted earnings of highly educated Americans have gone nowhere since the late 1990s.

An Inequality of Power

So what is really going on? Corporate profits have soared as a share of national income, but there is no sign of a rise in the rate of return on investment. How is that possible? Well, it's what you would expect if rising profits reflect monopoly power rather than returns to capital.

As for wages and salaries, never mind college degrees—all the big gains are going to a tiny group of individuals holding strategic positions in corporate suites or astride the crossroads of finance. Rising inequality isn't about who has the knowledge; it's about who has the power.

Now, there's a lot we could do to redress this inequality of power. We could levy higher taxes on corporations and the wealthy, and invest the proceeds in programs that help working families. We could raise the minimum wage and make it easier for workers to organize. It's not hard to imagine a truly serious effort to make America less unequal.

But given the determination of one major party to move policy in exactly the opposite direction, advocating such an effort makes you sound partisan. Hence the desire to see the whole thing as an education problem instead. But we should recognize that popular evasion for what it is: a deeply unserious fantasy.

> *"Postsecondary education is still our best ladder to the middle class, but it will remain a rickety one until more kids who begin the climb complete it."*

Higher Education Will Alleviate Inequality Only If It Is Affordable

Ronald Brownstein

In the following viewpoint, Ronald Brownstein argues that the rising costs of college create a barrier to access, stratifying class privilege. Brownstein claims that stagnant family income and rising tuition have forced low-income students to borrow more. Yet, he contends that many of these students fail to finish college and reap the economic rewards of an education. Brownstein is Atlantic Media's editorial director for strategic partnerships and author of The Second Civil War: How Extreme Partisanship Has Paralyzed Washington and Polarized America.

As you read, consider the following questions:

1. According to the author, what step did the federal government take in 1965 to improve low-income student access to a college education?

2. Brownstein claims that college students in the top one-fifth of incomes are how much more likely to graduate than students in the lower one-fifth?

3. According to the author, what four states are experimenting with linking state aid for higher education to student performance?

Since the seminal federal study "A Nation at Risk" launched the modern educational-reform movement in 1983, America's K–12 schools have faced persistent pressure for greater accountability and improved results. The reforms have been imperfect and the outcomes uneven, but the irreversible direction has been toward stiffening both expectations and consequences for what students achieve from elementary grades through high school.

The Federal Higher Education Policy

Over these stormy decades of "education wars," the nation's colleges and universities almost completely escaped similar scrutiny. "When it comes to higher education, we are really 25 years behind K–12 education, at least in accountability," says Michael Dannenberg, higher education director at the Education Trust, which advocates for low-income children.

But now, the accountability revolution that reshaped K–12 is reaching critical mass for the cap-and-gown set. From President [Barack] Obama and governors such as California's Jerry Brown to leading foundations and educators, more voices are insisting that postsecondary schools confront the intertwined problems of rising tuition, exploding student debt, and disappointing completion rates. "People are realizing, we [need] some way to get ... more bang for our buck," said Tom Kane, a Harvard professor of education and economics who advised a coalition of prominent educators and foundations that recently issued a reform blueprint called "The American Dream 2.0."

Dannenberg argues that federal higher education policy has progressed through three phases. With the creation of Pell Grants for lower-income students in 1965, Washington initially focused on expanding access. Later, a proliferation of tax credits and loan programs emphasized college affordability for families through the upper middle class. Obama has expanded Washington's commitment on both fronts, with big Pell Grant and tax credit increases and student loan reform. But, more than his predecessors, he is also widening Washington's focus to encompass completion and cost. "Taxpayers can't keep on subsidizing higher and higher and higher costs for higher education," the president insisted in his State of the Union address.

Recent Trends in College Cost and Completion

In higher education, as in health care, America boasts many of the world's best institutions but produces disappointing results overall. Access is improving: Since 1972, the share of low-income high school graduates who start college immediately has about doubled, to more than half, according to the National Center for Education Statistics. Yet nearly half of students who enroll in a postsecondary institution don't complete a degree within six years. For African Americans and Hispanics, the number is about three-fifths. Despite Washington's huge investment in access, since 1970 the gap in college completion rates between students from the bottom and top fifths of the income ladder has doubled. Those from the top fifth are now seven times more likely to graduate than those from the bottom.

The Rising Unaffordability of College

It used to be that students . . . could attend a public university and graduate with little or no debt. Then came the recession, when state governments slashed funding of higher education and families began paying higher tuition bills.

Now, even as the economy recovers . . . states have not restored their funding, and tuition keeps rising, leaving parents and students scrambling to cover costs.

Danielle Douglas-Gabriel,
"Going to a Public College Isn't as Affordable as It Used to Be,"
Washington Post, *January 30, 2015.*

Debt compounds the problem. Stagnant family incomes and rising tuition expenses—driven by both growing costs and shrinking state support for public colleges—have forced students to borrow twice as much annually as a decade ago. Student debt has soared past $1 trillion (outpacing credit card debt) and, as the Education Trust notes, low-income students are more likely to borrow, and less likely to finish, than higher-income classmates.

Education remains critical to reversing the erosion in upward mobility that has made it harder for kids born near the bottom to reach the top in the United States than in many European nations. Yet with these dispiriting trends in cost, completion, and debt, higher education arguably now serves more to stratify than to dissolve class privilege.

Initiatives to Increase Affordability

The debate is just developing over how to reverse these interlocked dynamics. Indiana, Ohio, Pennsylvania, and Tennessee are experimenting with linking state aid for higher education to student performance. Obama has proposed grant competitions for states and individual institutions to improve completion and affordability, and the administration has created a "scorecard" to track colleges' performance on those measures. The president is also urging Congress to incorporate schools' performance on affordability and value into the accreditation process that determines which institutions can receive federal student aid.

Both the Education Trust and the coalition that produced the "2.0" report would push harder on that lever by more directly tying federal aid to completion rates. Among other things, the coalition proposes to give students bigger Pell Grants if they take more credits (which aids completion) and to allow some states to divert student-aid dollars into comprehensive experiments to improve graduation rates. Kane says such tests eventually could guide federal changes, as state-level welfare reforms did in the 1990s.

The Education Trust recently issued the most visionary proposal: Consolidate virtually all federal student aid beyond Pell Grants into budget-neutral block grants for states that commit to providing debt-free higher education for low-income students and interest-free loans for middle-income students. Participating schools would be required to contain costs and boost graduation; students would need to maintain steady progress toward completion. It's a powerful conception of shared responsibility.

The sweeping changes these reports envision won't come anytime soon. But, like "A Nation at Risk," their message should inspire a lasting direction. Postsecondary education is still our best ladder to the middle class, but it will remain a rickety one until more kids who begin the climb complete it.

> *"For most of our nation's history, whatever the inequality in wealth between the richest and poorest citizens, we maintained a cultural equality known nowhere else in the world—for whites, anyway."*

Cultural Inequality Is the Problem That Needs to Be Addressed

Charles Murray

In the following viewpoint, Charles Murray argues that income inequality is not the problem in the United States; a decline in cultural equality is the problem. Murray claims that among white Americans there has been a cultural cleaving over the last couple decades, where shared values have disintegrated. He contends that the lack of shared values between today's wealthy, upper-middle-class and working-class populations is the real social problem, not the difference in income. Murray is W.H. Brady Scholar at the American Enterprise Institute for Public Policy Research and author of Coming Apart: The State of White America, 1960–2010.

As you read, consider the following questions:

1. What are the demographic characteristics of the two fictional towns Murray discusses, Belmont and Fishtown?

2. What was the average family income in 2000 in what Murray calls the Super ZIPs?

3. What role does Murray think that government and public policy should play in eliminating cultural inequality?

America is coming apart. For most of our nation's history, whatever the inequality in wealth between the richest and poorest citizens, we maintained a cultural equality known nowhere else in the world—for whites, anyway. "The more opulent citizens take great care not to stand aloof from the people," wrote Alexis de Tocqueville, the great chronicler of American democracy, in the 1830s. "On the contrary, they constantly keep on easy terms with the lower classes: They listen to them, they speak to them every day."

Americans love to see themselves this way. But there's a problem: It's not true anymore, and it has been progressively less true since the 1960s.

The Problem of Cultural Inequality

People are starting to notice the great divide. The Tea Party sees the aloofness in a political elite that thinks it knows best and orders the rest of America to fall in line. The Occupy movement [referring to the Occupy Wall Street movement, which protests against social and economic inequality] sees it in an economic elite that lives in mansions and flies on private jets. Each is right about an aspect of the problem, but that problem is more pervasive than either political or economic inequality. What we now face is a problem of cultural inequality.

When Americans used to brag about "the American way of life"—a phrase still in common use in 1960—they were talking about a civic culture that swept an extremely large proportion of Americans of all classes into its embrace. It was a culture encompassing shared experiences of daily life and shared assumptions about central American values involving marriage, honesty, hard work and religiosity.

Over the past 50 years, that common civic culture has unraveled. We have developed a new upper class with advanced educations, often obtained at elite schools, sharing tastes and preferences that set them apart from mainstream America. At the same time, we have developed a new lower class, characterized not by poverty but by withdrawal from America's core cultural institutions.

Belmont and Fishtown

To illustrate just how wide the gap has grown between the new upper class and the new lower class, let me start with the broader upper middle and working classes from which they are drawn, using two fictional neighborhoods that I hereby label Belmont (after an archetypal upper-middle-class suburb near Boston) and Fishtown (after a neighborhood in Philadelphia that has been home to the white working class since the [American] Revolution).

To be assigned to Belmont, the people in the statistical nationwide databases on which I am drawing must have at least a bachelor's degree and work as a manager, physician, attorney, engineer, architect, scientist, college professor or content producer in the media. To be assigned to Fishtown, they must have no academic degree higher than a high school diploma. If they work, it must be in a blue-collar job, a low-skill service job such as cashier, or a low-skill white-collar job such as mail clerk or receptionist.

People who qualify for my Belmont constitute about 20% of the white population of the U.S., ages 30 to 49. People who qualify for my Fishtown constitute about 30% of the white population of the U.S., ages 30 to 49.

I specify white, meaning non-Latino white, as a way of clarifying how broad and deep the cultural divisions in the U.S. have become. Cultural inequality is not grounded in race or ethnicity. I specify ages 30 to 49—what I call prime-age adults—to make it clear that these trends are not explained by changes in the ages of marriage or retirement.

In Belmont and Fishtown, here's what happened to America's common culture between 1960 and 2010.

The Changes to Family Structure

Marriage: In 1960, extremely high proportions of whites in both Belmont and Fishtown were married—94% in Belmont and 84% in Fishtown. In the 1970s, those percentages declined about equally in both places. Then came the great divergence. In Belmont, marriage stabilized during the mid-1980s, standing at 83% in 2010. In Fishtown, however, marriage continued to slide; as of 2010, a minority (just 48%) were married. The gap in marriage between Belmont and Fishtown grew to 35 percentage points, from just 10.

Single parenthood: Another aspect of marriage—the percentage of children born to unmarried women—showed just as great a divergence. Though politicians and media eminences are too frightened to say so, nonmarital births are problematic. On just about any measure of development you can think of, children who are born to unmarried women fare worse than the children of divorce and far worse than children raised in intact families. This unwelcome reality persists even after controlling for the income and education of the parents.

In 1960, just 2% of all white births were nonmarital. When we first started recording the education level of mothers in 1970, 6% of births to white women with no more than a high school education—women, that is, with a Fishtown education—were out of wedlock. By 2008, 44% were nonmarital. Among the college-educated women of Belmont, less than 6% of all births were out of wedlock as of 2008, up from 1% in 1970.

Males in the Workplace

Industriousness: The norms for work and women were revolutionized after 1960, but the norm for men putatively has remained the same: Healthy men are supposed to work. In practice, though, that norm has eroded everywhere. In Fishtown, the change has been drastic. (To avoid conflating this phenomenon with the latest recession, I use data collected in March 2008 as the end point for the trends.)

The primary indicator of the erosion of industriousness in the working class is the increase of prime-age males with no more than a high school education who say they are not available for work—they are "out of the labor force." That percentage went from a low of 3% in 1968 to 12% in 2008. Twelve percent may not sound like much until you think about the men we're talking about: in the prime of their working lives, their 30s and 40s, when, according to hallowed American tradition, every American man is working or looking for work. Almost one out of eight now aren't. Meanwhile, not much has changed among males with college educations. Only 3% were out of the labor force in 2008.

There's also been a notable change in the rates of less-than-full-time work. Of the men in Fishtown who had jobs, 10% worked fewer than 40 hours a week in 1960, a figure that grew to 20% by 2008. In Belmont, the number rose from 9% in 1960 to 12% in 2008.

Growth in Crime and an Increase in Secularism

Crime: The surge in crime that began in the mid-1960s and continued through the 1980s left Belmont almost untouched and ravaged Fishtown. From 1960 to 1995, the violent crime rate in Fishtown more than sextupled while remaining nearly flat in Belmont. The reductions in crime since the mid-1990s that have benefited the nation as a whole have been smaller in Fishtown, leaving it today with a violent crime rate that is still 4.7 times the 1960 rate.

Religiosity: Whatever your personal religious views, you need to realize that about half of American philanthropy, volunteering and associational memberships is directly church related, and that religious Americans also account for much more nonreligious social capital than their secular neighbors. In that context, it is worrisome for the culture that the U.S. as a whole has become markedly more secular since 1960, and especially worrisome that Fishtown has become much more secular than Belmont. It runs against the prevailing narrative of secular elites versus a working class still clinging to religion, but the evidence from the General Social Survey [GSS], the most widely used database on American attitudes and values, does not leave much room for argument.

For example, suppose we define "de facto secular" as someone who either professes no religion at all or who attends a worship service no more than once a year. For the early GSS surveys conducted from 1972 to 1976, 29% of Belmont and 38% of Fishtown fell into that category. Over the next three decades, secularization did indeed grow in Belmont, from 29% in the 1970s to 40% in the GSS surveys taken from 2006 to 2010. But it grew even more in Fishtown, from 38% to 59%.

The Isolation of the Upper Middle Class

It can be said without hyperbole that these divergences put Belmont and Fishtown into different cultures. But it's not just the working class that's moved; the upper middle class has pulled away in its own fashion, too.

If you were an executive living in Belmont in 1960, income inequality would have separated you from the construction worker in Fishtown, but remarkably little cultural inequality. You lived a more expensive life, but not a much different life. Your kitchen was bigger, but you didn't use it to prepare yogurt and muesli for breakfast. Your television screen was bigger, but you and the construction worker watched a lot of the same shows (you didn't have much choice). Your house might have had a den that the construction worker's lacked, but it had no StairMaster or lap pool, nor any gadget to monitor your percentage of body fat. You both drank Bud [Budweiser], Miller, Schlitz or Pabst [Blue Ribbon], and the phrase "boutique beer" never crossed your lips. You probably both smoked. If you didn't, you did not glare contemptuously at people who did.

When you went on vacation, you both probably took the family to the seashore or on a fishing trip, and neither involved hotels with five stars. If you had ever vacationed outside the U.S. (and you probably hadn't), it was a one-time trip to Europe, where you saw eight cities in 14 days—not one of the two or three trips abroad you now take every year for business, conferences or eco-vacations in the cloud forests of Costa Rica.

You both lived in neighborhoods where the majority of people had only high school diplomas—and that might well have included you. The people around you who did have college degrees had almost invariably gotten them at state universities or small religious colleges mostly peopled by students who were the first generation of their families to attend college. Except in academia, investment banking, a few foundations, the CIA [Central Intelligence Agency] and the State Department, you were unlikely to run into a graduate of Harvard, Princeton or Yale.

Even the income inequality that separated you from the construction worker was likely to be new to your adulthood.

The odds are good that your parents had been in the working class or middle class, that their income had not been much different from the construction worker's, that they had lived in communities much like his, and that the texture of the construction worker's life was recognizable to you from your own childhood.

The Rise of the Super ZIPs

Taken separately, the differences in lifestyle that now separate Belmont from Fishtown are not sinister, but those quirks of the upper middle class that I mentioned—the yogurt and muesli and the rest—are part of a mosaic of distinctive practices that have developed in Belmont. These have to do with the food Belmonters eat, their drinking habits, the ages at which they marry and have children, the books they read (and their number), the television shows and movies they watch (and the hours spent on them), the humor they enjoy, the way they take care of their bodies, the way they decorate their homes, their leisure activities, their work environments and their child-raising practices. Together, they have engendered cultural separation.

It gets worse. A subset of Belmont consists of those who have risen to the top of American society. They run the country, meaning that they are responsible for the films and television shows you watch, the news you see and read, the fortunes of the nation's corporations and financial institutions, and the jurisprudence, legislation and regulations produced by government. They are the new upper class, even more detached from the lives of the great majority of Americans than the people of Belmont—not just socially but spatially as well. The members of this elite have increasingly sorted themselves into hyper-wealthy and hyper-elite ZIP codes that I call the Super ZIPs.

In 1960, America already had the equivalent of Super ZIPs in the form of famously elite neighborhoods—places like the Upper East Side of New York, Philadelphia's Main Line, the

North Shore of Chicago and Beverly Hills. But despite their prestige, the people in them weren't uniformly wealthy or even affluent. Across 14 of the most elite places to live in 1960, the median family income wasn't close to affluence. It was just $84,000 (in today's purchasing power). Only one in four adults in those elite communities had a college degree.

By 2000, that diversity had dwindled. Median family income had doubled, to $163,000 in the same elite ZIP codes. The percentage of adults with BAs [bachelor of arts degrees] rose to 67% from 26%. And it's not just that elite neighborhoods became more homogeneously affluent and highly educated—they also formed larger and larger clusters.

If you are invited to a dinner party by one of Washington's power elite, the odds are high that you will be going to a home in Georgetown, the rest of northwest D.C., Chevy Chase, Bethesda, Potomac or McLean, comprising 13 adjacent ZIP codes in all. If you rank all the ZIP codes in the country on an index of education and income and group them by percentiles, you will find that 11 of these 13 D.C.-area ZIP codes are in the 99th percentile and the other two in the 98th. Ten of them are in the top half of the 99th percentile.

Similarly large clusters of Super ZIPs can be found around New York City, Los Angeles, the San Francisco–San Jose corridor, Boston and a few of the nation's other largest cities. Because running major institutions in this country usually means living near one of these cities, it works out that the nation's power elite does in fact live in a world that is far more culturally rarefied and isolated than the world of the power elite in 1960.

And the isolation is only going to get worse. Increasingly, the people who run the country were born into that world. Unlike the typical member of the elite in 1960, they have never known anything but the new upper-class culture. We are now seeing more and more third-generation members of the elite. Not even their grandparents have been able to give them a window into life in the rest of America.

The Formation of the New Classes

Why have these new lower and upper classes emerged? For explaining the formation of the new lower class, the easy explanations from the left don't withstand scrutiny. It's not that white working-class males can no longer make a "family wage" that enables them to marry. The average male employed in a working-class occupation earned as much in 2010 as he did in 1960. It's not that a bad job market led discouraged men to drop out of the labor force. Labor-force dropout increased just as fast during the boom years of the 1980s, 1990s and 2000s as it did during bad years.

As I've argued in much of my previous work, I think that the reforms of the 1960s jump-started the deterioration. Changes in social policy during the 1960s made it economically more feasible to have a child without having a husband if you were a woman or to get along without a job if you were a man; safer to commit crimes without suffering consequences; and easier to let the government deal with problems in your community that you and your neighbors formerly had to take care of.

But, for practical purposes, understanding why the new lower class got started isn't especially important. Once the deterioration was under way, a self-reinforcing loop took hold as traditionally powerful social norms broke down. Because the process has become self-reinforcing, repealing the reforms of the 1960s (something that's not going to happen) would change the trends slowly at best.

Meanwhile, the formation of the new upper class has been driven by forces that are nobody's fault and resist manipulation. The economic value of brains in the marketplace will continue to increase no matter what, and the most successful of each generation will tend to marry each other no matter what. As a result, the most successful Americans will continue to trend toward consolidation and isolation as a class. Changes in marginal tax rates on the wealthy won't make a difference. Increasing scholarships for working-class children won't make a difference.

The Solution

The only thing that can make a difference is the recognition among Americans of all classes that a problem of cultural inequality exists and that something has to be done about it. That "something" has nothing to do with new government programs or regulations. Public policy has certainly affected the culture, unfortunately, but unintended consequences have been as grimly inevitable for conservative social engineering as for liberal social engineering.

The "something" that I have in mind has to be defined in terms of individual American families acting in their own interests and the interests of their children. Doing that in Fishtown requires support from outside. There remains a core of civic virtue and involvement in working-class America that could make headway against its problems if the people who are trying to do the right things get the reinforcement they need—not in the form of government assistance, but in validation of the values and standards they continue to uphold. The best thing that the new upper class can do to provide that reinforcement is to drop its condescending "nonjudgmentalism." Married, educated people who work hard and conscientiously raise their kids shouldn't hesitate to voice their disapproval of those who defy these norms. When it comes to marriage and the work ethic, the new upper class must start preaching what it practices.

Changing life in the Super ZIPs requires that members of the new upper class rethink their priorities. Here are some propositions that might guide them: Life sequestered from anybody not like yourself tends to be self-limiting. Places to live in which the people around you have no problems that need cooperative solutions tend to be sterile. America outside the enclaves of the new upper class is still a wonderful place, filled with smart, interesting, entertaining people. If you're not part of that America, you've stripped yourself of much of what makes being American special.

Such priorities can be expressed in any number of familiar decisions: the neighborhood where you buy your next home, the next school that you choose for your children, what you tell them about the value and virtues of physical labor and military service, whether you become an active member of a religious congregation (and what kind you choose) and whether you become involved in the life of your community at a more meaningful level than charity events.

Everyone in the new upper class has the monetary resources to make a wide variety of decisions that determine whether they engage themselves and their children in the rest of America or whether they isolate themselves from it. The only question is which they prefer to do.

That's it? But where's my five-point plan? We're supposed to trust that large numbers of parents will spontaneously, voluntarily make the right choice for the country by making the right choice for themselves and their children?

Yes, we are, but I don't think that's naive. I see too many signs that the trends I've described are already worrying a lot of people. If enough Americans look unblinkingly at the nature of the problem, they'll fix it. One family at a time. For their own sakes. That's the American way.

Periodical and Internet Sources Bibliography

The following articles have been selected to supplement the diverse views presented in this chapter.

Max Borders	"Wealth Inequality: Predictably Irrational," *Freeman*, March 5, 2013.
Josh Freedman	"Why American Colleges Are Becoming a Force for Inequality," *Atlantic*, May 16, 2013.
Ron Haskins	"The Myth of the Disappearing Middle Class," *Washington Post*, March 29, 2012.
Robert Kuttner	"Education Alone Is Not the Answer to Income Inequality and Slow Recovery," *American Prospect*, August 14, 2014.
Norm Ornstein	"A Plan to Reduce Inequality: Give $1,000 to Every Newborn Baby," *Atlantic*, February 13, 2014.
Avik Roy	"The Biggest Reason for Income Inequality Is Single Parenthood," *Forbes*, November 19, 2014.
John Schmitt	"The Minimum Wage Is Too Damn Low," Center for Economic and Policy Research, March 2012.
George P. Shultz and Eric A. Hanushek	"Education Is the Key to a Healthy Economy," *Wall Street Journal*, April 30, 2012.
Nick Schulz	"Raising Minimum Wage Is Maximum Stupidity," *Boston Herald*, April 11, 2012.
Noah Smith	"How to Fix America's Wealth Inequality: Teach Americans to Be Cheap," *Atlantic*, March 12, 2013.
Walter E. Williams	"Income Inequality," *Townhall*, January 15, 2014.

For Further Discussion

Chapter 1

1. Richard A. Epstein contends that as long as there is a Pareto improvement in the economy, inequality is not a problem. How do you think Joseph E. Stiglitz would respond to Epstein? Explain.

2. John Tamny argues in favor of inequality as a force that lessens the lifestyle gap. Based on what Richard Wilkinson writes in his viewpoint, how do you think Wilkinson would respond to Tamny's argument? Explain.

Chapter 2

1. Drawing on at least two of the viewpoints in this chapter, explain why you think the gender wage gap either is or is not an indication of discrimination. What kind of evidence proves or disproves the existence of discrimination? Explain.

2. Arthur MacEwan cites figures that show income inequality between blacks and whites. Drawing upon the viewpoint of June E. O'Neill, who discusses the gender wage gap, are there any analogous choices that could explain the racial wage gap? Why, or why not?

Chapter 3

1. Zachary Karabell claims that redistributing income will not fundamentally change the problem of wage stagnation. If this is true, is there no reason to eliminate income inequality? Why, or why not?

2. Jeff Jacoby contends that poverty is correlated with single parenthood (and he notes, "Correlation isn't proof of causation, of course") but suggests that poverty could be re-

duced by marriage. Do you agree or disagree with his viewpoint? Explain your answer.

Chapter 4

1. David Azerrad and Rea S. Hederman Jr. argue that nothing needs to be done about income inequality because the rich did not get richer at the expense of the poor. How do you think Robert B. Reich would respond to their claim? Explain.

2. Paul Krugman claims that improving education will not solve the inequality problem since the problem is one of inequality of power. Drawing upon the viewpoints of Josh Kraushaar and Ronald Brownstein, how might a critic of Krugman reply that better education can help inequality of power? Explain your reasoning.

Organizations to Contact

The editors have compiled the following list of organizations concerned with the issues debated in this book. The descriptions are derived from materials provided by the organizations. All have publications or information available for interested readers. The list was compiled on the date of publication of the present volume; names, addresses, phone and fax numbers, and e-mail and Internet addresses may change. Be aware that many organizations take several weeks or longer to respond to inquiries, so allow as much time as possible.

American Association of University Women (AAUW)
1111 Sixteenth Street NW, Washington, DC   20036
(800) 326-2289 • fax: (202) 872-1425
e-mail: connect@aauw.org
website: www.aauw.org

The American Association of University Women (AAUW) promotes equity and education for women and girls. Through advocacy, education, and research, AAUW aims to support women in their careers and promote pay equity. AAUW publishes numerous reports, including "The Simple Truth About the Gender Pay Gap."

American Enterprise Institute for Public Policy Research (AEI)
1150 Seventeenth Street NW, Washington, DC   20036
(202) 862-5800 • fax: (202) 862-7177
e-mail: info@aei.org
website: www.aei.org

The American Enterprise Institute for Public Policy Research (AEI) is a private, nonpartisan, not-for-profit institution dedicated to research and education on issues of government, politics, economics, and social welfare. AEI sponsors research and publishes materials about defending the principles and improving the institutions of American freedom and democratic capitalism. Among AEI's publications is the online magazine the *American* and the book *Prices, Poverty, and Inequality: Why Americans Are Better Off than You Think.*

American Federation of Labor and Congress of Industrial Organizations (AFL-CIO)

815 Sixteenth Street NW, Washington, DC   20006
(202) 637-5000
website: www.aflcio.org

The American Federation of Labor and Congress of Industrial Organizations (AFL-CIO) is a voluntary federation of fifty-six national and international labor unions, representing 12.2 million members. The AFL-CIO educates union members about issues that affect the daily lives of working families and encourages them to make their voices heard by government. The AFL-CIO has numerous publications available at its website, including "Working America: Wealth Inequality Is Much Worse than You Think (and Congress Just Made It Worse)."

Cato Institute

1000 Massachusetts Avenue NW
Washington, DC   20001-5403
(202) 842-0200 • fax: (202) 842-3490
website: www.cato.org

The Cato Institute is a public policy research foundation dedicated to the principles of individual liberty, limited government, free markets, and peace. Its scholars and analysts conduct independent, nonpartisan research on a wide range of policy issues. Among its publications are the quarterly *Cato Journal*, the bimonthly *Cato Policy Report*, and *Policy Analysis* articles such as "Thinking Clearly About Economic Inequality."

Center for American Progress (CAP)

1333 H Street NW, 10th Floor, Washington, DC   20005
(202) 682-1611 • fax: (202) 682-1867
website: www.americanprogress.org

The Center for American Progress (CAP) is a nonprofit, non-partisan organization dedicated to improving the lives of Americans through progressive ideas and action. CAP dialogues with leaders, thinkers, and citizens to explore the vital issues facing America and the world. CAP publishes numerous research papers that are available at its website, including "The Impact of Inequality on Growth."

Center for Economic and Policy Research (CEPR)

1611 Connecticut Avenue NW, Suite 400
Washington, DC   20009
(202) 293-5380 • fax: (202) 588-1356
e-mail: info@cepr.net
website: www.cepr.net

The Center for Economic and Policy Research (CEPR) aims to promote democratic debate on the most important economic and social issues that affect people's lives. CEPR conducts both professional research and public education. CEPR provides briefings and testimony to Congress and reports for the general public, including "Inequality as Policy: The United States Since 1979."

Center on Budget and Policy Priorities (CBPP)

820 First Street NE, Suite 510, Washington, DC   20002
(202) 408-1080 • fax: (202) 408-1056
e-mail: center@cbpp.org
website: www.cbpp.org

The Center on Budget and Policy Priorities (CBPP) is a policy organization working at the federal and state levels on fiscal policy and public programs that affect low- and moderate-income families and individuals. CBPP conducts research and analysis to inform public debates over proposed budget and tax policies. Many reports are available on CBPP's website, including "A Guide to Statistics on Historical Trends in Income Inequality."

Economic Policy Institute (EPI)

1333 H Street NW, Suite 300, East Tower
Washington, DC   20005-4707
(202) 775-8810 • fax: (202) 775-0819
e-mail: epi@epi.org
website: www.epi.org

The Economic Policy Institute (EPI) is a nonprofit think tank that seeks to broaden the discussion about economic policy to include the interests of low- and middle-income workers. EPI briefs policy makers at all levels of government; provides technical support to national, state, and local activists and community organizations; testifies before national, state, and local legislatures; and provides information and background to the print and electronic media. EPI publishes books, studies, issue briefs, popular education materials, and other publications, among which is its flagship publication "The State of Working America," the full text of which is available online.

Institute for Women's Policy Research (IWPR)

1200 Eighteenth Street NW, Suite 301, Washington, DC   20036
(202) 785-5100 • fax: (202) 833-4362
e-mail: iwpr@iwpr.org
website: www.iwpr.org

The Institute for Women's Policy Research (IWPR) conducts research and disseminates its findings to address the needs of women, promote public dialogue, and strengthen families, communities, and societies. With initiatives on the topics of education, democracy, poverty, work, and health, IWPR aims to promote gender equity. IWPR publishes numerous reports and briefing papers, including "Pay Secrecy and Wage Discrimination."

United for a Fair Economy (UFE)

62 Summer Street, Boston, MA   02110
(617) 423-2148 • fax: (617) 423-0191
e-mail: info@faireconomy.org
website: www.faireconomy.org

United for a Fair Economy (UFE) aims to raise awareness that concentrated wealth and power undermine the economy, corrupt democracy, deepen the racial divide, and tear communities apart. UFE supports and helps build social movements for greater equality through projects such as its Racial Wealth Divide program. UFE has numerous resources available at its website, including reports and infographics.

Urban Institute

2100 M Street NW, Washington, DC   20037
(202) 833-7200
website: www.urban.org

The Urban Institute works to foster sound public policy and effective government by gathering data, conducting research, evaluating programs, and educating Americans on social and economic issues. The Urban Institute builds knowledge about the nation's social and fiscal challenges through evidence-based research meant to diagnose problems and figure out which policies and programs work best. The Urban Institute publishes policy briefs, commentary, and research reports, including "Less than Equal: Racial Disparities in Wealth Accumulation."

Bibliography of Books

Orazio P.
Attanasio, Erich
Battistin, and
Mario Padula
Inequality in Living Standards Since 1980: Income Tells Only a Small Part of the Story. Washington, DC: AEI Press, 2010.

Francine D. Blau
Gender, Inequality, and Wages. New York: Oxford University Press, 2012.

Jim Clifton
The Coming Jobs War: What Every Leader Must Know About the Future of Job Creation. New York: Gallup Press, 2011.

Chuck Collins
99 to 1: How Wealth Inequality Is Wrecking the World and What We Can Do About It. San Francisco, CA: Berrett-Koehler Publishers, 2012.

Uri Dadush,
Kemal Dervis,
Sarah Puritz
Milsom, and
Bennett Stancil
Inequality in America: Facts, Trends, and International Perspectives. Washington, DC: Brookings Institution Press, 2012.

Peter Edelman
So Rich, So Poor: Why It's So Hard to End Poverty in America. New York: New Press, 2012.

Steve Fraser
The Age of Acquiescence: The Life and Death of American Resistance to Organized Wealth and Power. New York: Little, Brown and Company, 2015.

Howard Steven Friedman	*The Measure of a Nation: How to Regain America's Competitive Edge and Boost Our Global Standing.* Amherst, NY: Prometheus Books, 2012.
Diana Furchtgott-Roth	*Women's Figures: An Illustrated Guide to the Economic Progress of Women in America.* Washington, DC: AEI Press, 2012.
Jacob S. Hacker and Paul Pierson	*Winner-Take-All Politics: How Washington Made the Rich Richer—and Turned Its Back on the Middle Class.* New York: Simon & Schuster, 2010.
David Cay Johnston, ed.	*Divided: The Perils of Our Growing Inequality.* New York: New Press, 2014.
Lilly Ledbetter and Lanier Scott Isom	*Grace and Grit: My Fight for Equal Pay and Fairness at Goodyear and Beyond.* New York: Crown Archetype, 2012.
Leslie McCall	*The Undeserving Rich: American Beliefs About Inequality, Opportunity, and Redistribution.* New York: Cambridge University Press, 2013.
Branko Milanovic	*The Haves and the Have-Nots: A Brief and Idiosyncratic History of Global Inequality.* New York: Basic Books, 2011.

Brian Miller and Mike Lapham — *The Self-Made Myth: And the Truth About How Government Helps Individuals and Businesses Succeed.* San Francisco, CA: Berrett-Koehler Publishers, 2012.

Timothy Noah — *The Great Divergence: America's Growing Inequality Crisis and What We Can Do About It.* New York: Bloomsbury Press, 2012.

June O'Neill and Dave O'Neill — *The Declining Importance of Race and Gender in the Labor Market: The Role of Employment Discrimination Policies.* Washington, DC: AEI Press, 2012.

Robert D. Putnam — *Our Kids: The American Dream in Crisis.* New York: Simon & Schuster, 2015.

Robert B. Reich — *Aftershock: The Next Economy and America's Future.* New York: Vintage Books, 2011.

Robert B. Reich — *Beyond Outrage: What Has Gone Wrong with Our Economy and Our Democracy, and How to Fix It.* New York: Vintage Books, 2012.

Tavis Smiley and Cornel West — *The Rich and the Rest of Us: A Poverty Manifesto.* New York: Smiley Books, 2012.

Joseph E. Stiglitz — *The Price of Inequality: How Today's Divided Society Endangers Our Future.* New York: W.W. Norton, 2012.

Matt Taibbi

The Divide: American Injustice in the Age of the Wealth Gap. New York: Spiegel & Grau Trade Paperbacks, 2014.

Elizabeth Warren

A Fighting Chance. New York: Metropolitan Books, 2014.

Richard Wilkinson and Kate Pickett

The Spirit Level: Why Greater Equality Makes Societies Stronger. New York: Bloomsbury Press, 2010.

Index

A

Advanced degrees. *See* Higher educational attainment

Africa, 15

African American college students, 192

African American workers
  earning and income disparities, 73, 75, 109–112, 115
  wealth disparities, 113, 114–119, 117t

Alienation and isolation
  lower classes, 36–37, 64–66, 197
  upper classes, 203–204, 204–205, 205–206

"American Dream"
  current realities/dream at risk, 18, 19, 28, 36, 172–173
  education reform, 191–192
  national identity, 36
  qualities, 170
  unthreatened by income inequality, 167, 175
  See also Economic and social mobility

American pragmatism and values, 37–38, 165–166, 196–197, 206

Anti-discrimination laws
  civil rights, 69, 102
  gender and labor, 69–70, 97, 101–102

Antitrust laws, 34, 165

Arab Spring movement, 37

Armed Forces Qualification Test, 99

Asian American workers and earnings, 73, 75

Astor, John Jacob, 178

Azerrad, David, 167–175

B

Bailey, Ronald, 141–145

Bailouts, finance industry, 34, 62

Bartels, Larry, 51–52

Becker, Gary S., 24

Bernstein, Jared, 133

Black workers. *See* African American workers

Blau, Francine D., 96, 106

Blinder, Alan, 23

Boehner, John, 142

Bonica, Adam, 51

Booker, Cory, 183

Bowles, Erskine, 186

Brandeis, Louis, 158–159

Brenner, Reuven, 60

Brown, Jerry, 191

Brownstein, Ronald, 190–194

Buckley, Christopher, 60

Buffett, Warren, 171

Burtless, Gary, 15–16, 53–57

Bush, George H.W., 25

Bush, George W., 25, 163

C

Campaign finance deregulation, 34–35, 140, 165

Canada, 28

Capital gains taxes, 21, 25, 35, 164

protections for low and middle incomes, 53, 55–56, 56–57
taxing vs. borrowing, wars, 35
unaccounted, Gini index measurement, 15–16
US history, 25, 42, 44, 49, 51, 54, 163
Technological change, 169
education and skill levels of labor, 23–24
innovations and lifestyles, 60–61
productivity increases and jobs replaced, 33, 138, 159–160, 187
Technology infrastructure and tools, 29, 33
Temporary Assistance for Needy Families (TANF), 27, 118
Thiel, Peter, 187
Tocqueville, Alexis de, 37, 196
Tomasi, John, 177–178
Top 1
. *See* "The One Percent"
"Trickle-down behaviorism," 35–36
"Trickle-down consumption," 138–139
"Trickle-down economics," 31, 36–37, 163
Tuition. *See under* Higher educational attainment
Two-parent vs. one-parent families, 146–150, 198–199, 204
Tyson, Laura, 136–140

U

Unemployment
benefits, 27, 55, 154

minimum wage and, 45
named cause of income inequality, 122
national unrest, 36
United States, 36, 45, 199
youth, 36, 188
Unions. *See under* Labor
United Kingdom, 28, 64
University education. *See* Higher educational attainment
Upper middle class, 200–202
Upward mobility. *See* Economic and social mobility
Urban education, 181, 182–183
US Census Bureau, data collection, 14–15, 15–16, 56–57, 156–157
US Department of Commerce, 40
USA Today, income inequality surveys, 122–123, 153–154

V

Voter turnout
alienation, youth, 36–37
income level differences, 50t, 52
Voting rights, 165

W

Wage disparity. *See* Gender income disparity; Income inequality; Racial and ethnic income disparity
Wall Street. *See* Financial industry
War and society, 35–36
Warren, Elizabeth, 181
Washington Center for Equitable Growth, 173